PARA

INSIDE THE PARACHUTE REGIMENT

CLAIRE GILLMAN

Photographs by SIMON WALKER

P A R A

INSIDE THE PARACHUTE REGIMENT

CLAIRE GILLMAN

Photographs by SIMON WALKER

First published in Great Britain
1993
Bloomsbury Publishing Limited,
2 Soho Square, London W1V 5DE

A CIP catalogue record for this
book is available from the British
Library

ISBN 0 7475 1500 X

10 9 8 7 6 5 4 3 2 1

Designed by Bradbury and
Williams
Typeset by Florencetype Limited,
Kewstoke, Avon

Printed and bound in Hong Kong by Dah Hua Printing Co.

To my husband, Nick.
And, to Frances.

What manner of men are these who wear the maroon beret?

They are, firstly, all volunteers, and are toughened by hard physical training. As a result, they have that infectious optimism and that offensive eagerness which comes from physical well-being.

They have jumped from the air and, by doing so, have conquered fear.

Their duty lies in the van of battle: they are proud of their honour, and have never failed in any task.

They have the highest standards in all things, whether it be skill in battle or smartness in execution of all peacetime duties.

They have shown themselves to be as tenacious and determined in defence as they are courageous in attack.

They are, in fact, men apart.

Every man an emperor.

Field Marshal Montgomery of Alamein

AUTHOR'S NOTE
Despite every assistance from the
Parachute Regiment and 5
Airborne Brigade, the views
expressed in this book are entirely
my own or those of people who
were interviewed. They do not
necessarily reflect official
regimental or army policy.

PREFACE

My first introduction to the Parachute Regiment came when I was editing *Fitness* magazine. To motivate our readers, I wanted to carry a feature on the hardest fitness training programme in the country and the Parachute Regiment's selection course immediately sprang to mind. After approaching the relevant authorities and gaining the necessary permission, I duly turned up at Depot Para in Aldershot one cold and wintry morning for the start of the infamous 'P Company' test week. Although the Colonel had assured me that the regiment was very keen and happy to meet the press, the men were obviously not quite so eager. They made no disguise of the fact that they thought sending a female reporter to cover P Company was a very poor idea and I was met with a wave of 'not-another-journalist' nonchalance.

On taking the assignment, I suppose I had assumed that I would be treated with kid gloves but this was not the case. Although I was always treated with the utmost politeness, it was clear that I was expected to pitch in and have a go. If I couldn't keep up (which was usually the case), I had to jump in the back of a Land Rover pretty quickly or else be left behind.

On my third day with the regiment, after we had climbed the highest mountain in South Wales, there was a brief lunchbreak before the recruits started the next climb. During this respite, the Regimental Sergeant Major offered me a regulation doorstep spam sandwich, not knowing I was a vegetarian at the time. I declined. Notebook poised, I asked him, 'What happens to vegetarians in the army, Sergeant Major?' After a short pause, he replied, 'They die, ma'am.' He didn't smile and I was never quite sure just how serious he was.

Once published, the magazine article was extremely well received by the readers and, to my great delight, by the Parachute Regiment as well. Both Simon Walker, the photographer, and I felt that there was a great deal more material to be covered. Regimental Headquarters agreed and so this book was planned. We were given unprecedented access to every aspect of regimental and 5 Airborne Brigade life.

Over a period of eighteen months, Simon and I accompanied different elements of the brigade on trips ranging from bleak patrols of South Armagh to the steamy jungle of Central America. On every occasion, whether it was a nerve-wracking first balloon jump or at the end of a long and sleepless exercise, the Paras' distinctive black sense of humour always managed to raise a laugh. It played an important part in making our time with the brigade entertaining and enjoyable. Even in rare off-duty moments, we were invited to relax and share a joke with the men, whether it be at a raucous drink up in one of the favoured pubs in Aldershot or in the full ceremony of a regimental dinner night.

Throughout our time with the Paras, both Simon and I had to earn any popularity or respect that we received. By demonstrating that we were game to have a go at most things, even if we made a complete pig's ear of it, the officers and men cautiously warmed to us and we gradually gained acceptance.

Some people questioned the wisdom of using a female journalist for a book on such a manifestly macho subject. Certainly, there was no way I or, I suspect, any other woman could compete in physical terms but this fact worked in my favour – I posed no threat. Airborne soldiers judge outsiders

(and each other) extremely harshly and a male journalist would have had to prove himself in areas where I was not viewed competitively. As it was, once I had been accepted and was a familiar face, some men confided things in me which they perhaps would not have shared with another man.

Undoubtedly, the military world is largely misunderstood by civilians, and airborne forces in particular are quite content for such misconceptions to remain intact. They operate in an élitist, closed world and do not feel the need to explain themselves or their actions to anyone. Even other elements of the forces (whom the Paras refer to as 'crap hats') find them insufferably superior, but this only fuels the élitist mythology.

Airborne isolationism is not sought intentionally but is rather a result of complete autonomy born of an acute pride in the regiment. Airborne soldiers really do not need anyone else. They live in a closeknit fraternity where there is not only a great mutual liking but also a mutual respect. The sharing of

Blisters are a perennial problem for the speed-marching Paras; hot weather conditions simply compound the situation.

common experiences in the face of great adversity builds an *esprit de corps* which is hard for outsiders to understand or penetrate. Despite all indications to the contrary and accusations of excessive behaviour, within their fellowship there is a code of conduct and of honour which is very special, understood and adhered to by all.

Before spending time with 5 Airborne, I considered all soldiers much the same and held many of the same misconceptions as other civilians. However, having spent time in the company of Paras, I now have the utmost respect and liking for these robust men. They consistently display exceptional qualities, often in difficult situations, and are a fine example of a professional, élite fighting force. It is a rare privilege for outsiders to have an insight into their private world.

P Company staff exchange a joke and grab a quick cup of 'NATO Standard' - tea with two sugars - before starting their second gruelling mountain ascent in one morning.

INTRODUCTION

Military parachuting is a relatively recent form of warfare although the parachute itself has been in use since the late eighteenth century. During the two world wars parachutes and parachuting techniques were improved by enthusiasts and military air services for aircrew safety. However, it was not until 1936 that the potential of airborne troops was recognised when the Germans began to raise a parachute force; this became a *corps d'élite* of their expanding military forces and it was used to good effect in May 1940 when Germany unleashed its blitzkrieg campaign. During the overrun of Western Europe, German parachute and glider-borne troops seized important fortifications and objectives which might otherwise have caused critical delays to the advancing Panzer formations.

Inspired by the successes of the German airborne arm, Prime Minister Winston Churchill called for 'the formation of a Corps of at least 5,000 parachute troops' in June 1940. To this end, an experimental centre was set up at Ringway Airport, Manchester, and the men of 2 Commando received parachute training, with the first descents being made in July 1940. After several name changes, the unit became the 1st Parachute Battalion on 15 September 1941.

During 1941, several airborne raids were attempted with mixed results. Meanwhile, as the parachute battalions grew, corps and arms units (both parachute and glider-borne) were raised to support the infantry while experiments with equipment and techniques continued.

In early 1942 the Parachute Battalion received its first battle honour, at Bruneval, where a raid on a radar station secured important equipment and technicians. Later that year, on 1 August, the Parachute Regiment was formed officially and became the hub of the 1st Airborne Division.

Throughout the war years, airborne forces were involved in many actions, the two most epic of which are still commemorated annually. The first of these was in September 1944 when the unsupported 1st Airborne Division seized and held the bridge over the Rhine at Arnhem for nine days against major elements of a German SS Panzer Corps, and all units

Safe landings at Brize Norton. Note the bergen rope attached.

After a strenuous and
exhausting march, it is
far harder to be a good
shot than it is on the
range. 'March and shoot'
exercises are a realistic
test of soldiering skills.

distinguished themselves. Of the 10,095 men who landed,
fewer than 3,000 returned across the river.

The second, Rhine Crossing (Op Varsity) in March 1945,
represents the most successful and final major airborne
operation of the war when all objectives and the link-up with
ground forces were achieved within twenty-four hours.

It was during these war years that the men of the Airborne
Division earned the name '*Rote Teufel*' or 'Red Devils' from
their German opponents. Accepted as a compliment, the name
remains to this day the unofficial title of British airborne forces.

During the post-war years, the 'Red Devils' continued to
distinguish themselves. They have been involved in the
settling of unrest and conflicts all over the world, including:
Palestine (1945–8), the Middle East (1951–4), Cyprus (1956),
Suez (1956), Jordan (1958), Persian Gulf (1961–7), Radfan
(1964), Borneo (1965), British Guiana (1965–6), Aden (1967),
Anguilla (1969) and Northern Ireland (1969–90). Their most
recent honours were achieved in the Falklands campaign in
1982 where they were involved in the attacks on San Carlos,
Darwin, Goose Green, Mount Longdon, Wireless Ridge and
Port Stanley.

During its illustrious history, the brigade (all that remains of
the original division) has been through many transformations,
eventually emerging in its present form of 5 Airborne Brigade
on 14 November 1983.

**A Company commander
thinks of tactics while
on exercise in Cyprus.**

1
TRAINING AND P COMPANY
EARNING THE RED BERET

Airborne soldiers are the élite fighting force of armies all over the world. Their tough selection cadres and reputation on the battlefield precede their name and they are grudgingly respected, envied and often disliked by the rest of the British Army. An almost palpable *esprit de corps* perpetuates the élitist image still further and it is small wonder that applications to join this celebrated band of fighting men are

A brisk pace is kept up along the ridge of Fan Fawr in Brecon.

never in short supply despite the demographic depression which caused recruiting headaches for other elements of the services before recent Government defence (personnel) cuts.

There are two routes to earning the coveted red beret and becoming an airborne soldier. The more direct method is to join the Parachute Regiment as a recruit and follow the sixteen-week training programme before taking Pre-Parachute Selection (PPS, more commonly known as P Company), eventually joining a battalion. The alternative is to apply for All Arms P Company while serving with one of the other units in 5 Airborne Brigade. Either way, the standard for selection is extremely high and to succeed requires complete determination and dedication in the face of enormous physical and mental adversity.

For the seventeen- and eighteen-year-old recruits joining straight from a civilian background, a rapid re-education programme awaits them. There are lessons in the necessary soldiering skills of drill, handling of equipment and weapons, guard duties, radio procedures and so on, but equally important is mastery of the unwritten protocol of military life. Recruits very quickly learn the Who's Who of the army world and how to address members of the regiment, particularly those with whom they have daily contact. If they do not display the correct etiquette, they are very quickly brought up short by the staff, who have no truck with what they consider to be insolence. A standard quarter-inch haircut severs links still further with old and familiar civilian ways, and to encourage recruits to adapt and accept their new and sometimes baffling military life, contact with family and friends is restricted to the telephone for the first five weeks.

They are not trained to be mindless automatons, which is a commonly held misconception by the public. In fact, Parachute Regiment soldiers are selected from the top two intelligence grades of all army recruits. However, soldiers are conditioned to react promptly on a command, which is often confused with mindlessness. A soldier who cannot act on his own initiative is a great danger to himself and his colleagues, yet it is imperative that he reacts quickly and efficiently to a command despite the perils that such action may incur.

Throughout training, the schedule builds up progressively so that the recruits are at the peak of physical fitness for the P Company test week. It is unlikely that these men will ever be that fit again although strength and stamina are honed in the battalion as they get older. It is, in fact, the psychological pressure that is the biggest barrier to success for many recruits. Faced with a failure rate of 75 per cent and the certain knowledge that they have got to go through it all again if they do not pass first time, it takes a great deal of mental tenacity and belief in self to overcome the odds. Certain of the test week events have become legendary for their degree of difficulty and it is the prospect of these barriers which sometimes defeats a recruit before he even gets to the event.

Platoon staff who work closely with the recruits throughout their training period are keen to get as many good men through the selection as possible. Clichéd quotes such as 'I'm your mother now' from burly sergeants abound, but this is not so far from the truth since the recruits do not see their families during the early training period and have only fellow trainees or staff to turn to if they have a problem. As long as platoon staff consider the recruit is giving his all, they are hugely supportive and if there is a particular area of weakness, the recruit will probably receive extra tuition and help to give him a chance of passing. If platoon staff suspect that a recruit has the wrong attitude, irrespective of his physical ability, he will not receive any sympathy. Even if a recruit gets the required number of points on test week to pass, he can still be failed on attitude.

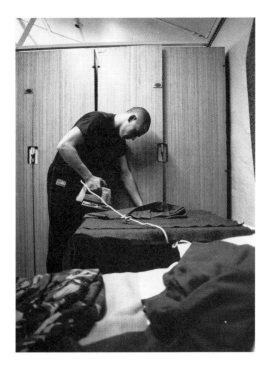

A recruit learning to live without Mother.

IT DOESN'T
TAKE A
MINUTE
TO BLEED
TO DEATH

First-day checking-in at Aldershot.

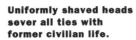

Uniformly shaved heads sever all ties with former civilian life.

CSM Warner - an archetypal Paratrooper and a classic Sergeant Major for P Company.

Humour is used to good effect throughout the training both to lighten an arduous physical ordeal and to toughen and quicken up the senses of the new arrivals. Quick wit and repartee are an important part of the regimental character. Previously shared common experiences under exceptional stress during training and the fact that everyone in the regiment, including officers, has been through the same gruelling experiences to earn their berets create a unity that is very potent. Naturally, the recruits want to be part of this team spirit and so the confidence and pride in the regiment shown by staff acts as a huge incentive to the young recruit. Until he has earned the right to be treated as an equal by passing PPS, a recruit is nothing more than that, and all are known as Joe Crow (or Joe for short) until their place in the regiment and thus an identity is earned. Often the staff will be sitting in their office drinking tea and, if they need an errand running, they will call for a 'body' and all the Joes within hearing distance are expected to rush forward saying 'let it be me'. Degrading perhaps, but indicative of how lowly recruits are regarded until they have passed P Company.

TRAINING In addition to soldiering skills, the recruits must immediately start a strenuous physical training programme that will prepare them for the series of arduous tests in the thirteenth week, namely P Company. According to one member of staff, 'The objectives of the physical training syllabus are to develop team spirit and character, strength, speed, agility and endurance. An emphasis is placed on marching with weight and running training although the programme is augmented with swimming, gym work, battle PT (assault course, steeplechase etc.) and team games such as football, volleyball and basketball.'

During the first week, each recruit must pass the Basic Fitness Test (BFT) as used by all units of the army. It consists

Recruits have twelve weeks in which to get as fit as possible for the test that awaits them.

of running one and a half miles in under fifteen minutes wearing training shoes. However, P Company recruits are expected unofficially to run it in about nine minutes. They must also undergo an Army Physical Fitness Assessment (AFTA) and from the combined results of this, the Physical Training Instructors (PTIs), known as PT Busters, can determine and adapt the training programme. At the same time, recruits are introduced to gym work including circuit training, jumping and landing from heights, balance and obstacle courses to improve agility and upper body strength. As the syllabus progresses, the recruits complete three- to six-mile runs in training shoes.

Over the next few weeks, training is complemented with speed marches, known as tabbing in the regiment, from the acronym TAB – tactical advance to battle – during which boots are worn and weight is added. The Parachute Regiment is the only unit in the army which places such a high emphasis on running in boots – the practice has been dropped by most other units. The recruits must complete a total of twenty-four tabs progressing to a distance of ten miles in one hour fifty minutes while carrying 35lb on their backs and a 7lb weapon, and wearing a heavy helmet. There are also regular sessions on the assault course and steeplechase in preparation for two of the tests at the beginning of P Company week.

The goal of the red beret is a great incentive to all recruits. Staff recognise this fact and use it well to overcome problems and get the best from their men even when they appear exhausted and believe they cannot go on. The principle that 'fear of failure must be greater than fear of the apparatus or task', as one member of staff put it, produces extraordinary performances on occasions and is definitely a great motivator when it comes to the trainasium in the fifth week of training.

The trainasium is a 44-foot-high structure (equivalent to a

three-storey building) made up of scaffolding poles, shuffle bars, see-saw planks, ropes and leap nets. A series of agility exercises and tests of nerve, such as touching the toes while in the middle of the highest shuffle bars, are carried out on the apparatus under the guidance and instruction of the staff. It is used to increase courage and confidence and to accustom the men to working on the command 'GO', ready for the aircraft. Recruits often freeze on the trainasium or try and bend down to steady themselves. For this, they are vigorously heckled and berated by the staff. Occasionally, someone will fall off. Serious injury is rare but always at the back of the mind of the recruits is the now legendary story of the fatality which occurred on the trainasium long ago. If someone should fall or get down, they are usually sent straight back up to complete the exercise and the staff use typically black regimental humour to reduce the tension with quips such as, 'Don't worry about falling, the ground will stop you' or 'If you do fall, hang on to the grass to stop you bouncing.'

At the end of their seventh week, the recruits are taken to Brecon in Wales for an introduction to tactical field training. They are taught and practise living in the field, individual navigation skills, endurance marching, the orders process, and recce and fighting patrols by day and night. By this time there will have been losses along the way. Some will have been sent back for retraining or held back due to injury, others will transfer out of the Paras, a few may leave the army completely. But the eighth week is the cut-off point; after this the recruits are committed to putting all their efforts into earning their red berets, and if they do not give a bare minimum of 100 per cent commitment, they will be rejected by the staff. One P Company sergeant major pointed out that 'some recruits benefit from failing the first time and in going through it again. They learn something about themselves and are stronger for it.'

Nonetheless, it is a bitter disappointment for those that do not make the grade on their first attempt.

On returning from Wales, the recruits enter the most intensive period of physical training as they build up their physical and mental endurance for P Company. They are introduced to approach marches which cover seventeen miles over rough terrain, and work closely with the platoon staff to strengthen any areas of perceived weakness.

The robust life that the recruit has led since his inauguration and the humour of the staff will have instilled in him a general toughness and confidence; when he gets to P Company, he will have a different mentality from when he arrived. At the end of twelve weeks of single-minded preparation, all the recruits should be ready for the gruelling test week which lies ahead.

P COMPANY A P Company sergeant major described test week as 'primarily a test that allows staff to ensure that a recruit has achieved the necessary level of fitness, character and determination at week thirteen of training before allowing him to continue further and ultimately to join the Parachute Regiment. It is such an enormous challenge to the recruit that, once overcome, it will strengthen his personal confidence and pride in the regiment. It is a vital link in the overall make-up of a Parachute Regiment soldier.' There have been many moves from external quarters to modify or drop P Company but these are always resisted by the regiment who put great store by their highly specialised training. Depot Para, where historically recruits have undergone training, moved from Aldershot (home of the Parachute Regiment) in Autumn 1992 but P Company remains the same.

DAY 1: Initially, recruits are introduced to P Company staff who will be assessing their performance throughout the test week and will lead them on every event, although they will still be accompanied by the platoon staff who have nurtured them from their arrival at barracks. Despite the seemingly harsh treatment of recruits hitherto, the platoon staff are immensely proprietorial of their recruits and they want the best results for them.

P Company starts on a Friday morning with a two-mile steeplechase across a rough country route that is littered with obstacles. It is dirty and unpleasant and definitely favours the slighter built men since they tend to be quicker, and this test is against the clock. By no means easy, it is nonetheless a fairly

Momentary relief as another event is successfully completed, but there are many more challenges to come before this recruit earns his red beret.

'Telling off' at the end of the steeplechase.

moderate introduction to the week in comparison with the second event of the morning, the log race.

This event is legendary among the men and however tough they may be, it is remembered with respect. The race involves carrying a 130lb log by toggle ropes in teams of eight men across one and a half miles of rough terrain. The course runs up and down steep hills all the way and is incredibly arduous. The rough ground coupled with trying to run as a team down narrow ravines makes it all too easy for recruits to lose their footing and fall. Once a recruit has 'fallen off the log', it is almost impossible for him to catch up and regain his position. The log is a dead weight to drag up the hill and its momentum downhill pulls the recruits faster than the loose ground dictates. Invariably, several recruits fail at this early obstacle and are back-squadded for further training. Those who fall receive no compassion from P Company staff, quite the opposite, and they are immediately separated from their colleagues who remain on the course. Many will receive a sympathetic word from their platoon commander in private before being returned for retraining but in public they are disgraced. The general attitude is that a recruit is not worthy of consideration for the regiment until he can prove that he is made of sterner stuff.

That afternoon, the milling takes place. This is a one-minute toe-to-toe boxing-type confrontation wearing 16oz gloves. The recruits are expected to sustain sixty seconds of controlled aggression and to throw as many punches as possible while still moving forward. The makeshift ring is made up of other recruits awaiting their turn on benches and the bout is refereed by a trained member of the PT Corps. No real damage can be done with gloves of this weight; milling is more a test of courage and tenacity than of boxing skills. Often the winner is not the most proficient pugilist but the man who keeps going in the face of a real hiding. Staff are watching for a recruit's reaction

The log race is one of the toughest events of the test week. If a recruit 'falls off the log', it is extremely hard for him to regain his place and this usually means an early failure.

when he is hurting and points are awarded for a win, draw or loss. Members of staff not closely involved with the event often come to watch the milling out of a macabre fascination for fighting which the PTIs find hard to understand.

A welcome weekend break is now in store for the recruits, which affords them a chance to prepare for the events ahead and to gather their kit together. They receive rousing speeches from their platoon staff and generally make every effort to psyche themselves up for the coming challenge.

Men rarely receive anything worse than a bloody nose during the milling. P Company staff are looking for mental tenacity and the ability to keep trying and coming forward even when it's beginning to hurt.

The milling is more a means of assessing a recruit's courage and aggression when taking a hammering than a test of his boxing skills.

DAY 2: There is a gruelling start to the week with a ten-mile route march off and on road, set at a cracking pace. Carrying 35lb packs on their backs and a 7lb weapon, the recruits must complete the course in one hour fifty minutes if they are to be allowed to continue. This is a very hard target to achieve and it means doubling (running) more than half the route. Recruits often fail on this event.

Immediately after finishing the ten-mile tab, while still exhausted, the recruits undergo a half-hour confidence test on the 44-foot-high trainasium. It is rare for recruits to fail on this event, particularly if they have trained extensively on it before, but there is always the risk of falling off or a loss of nerve so it still remains a challenge.

The afternoon brings with it the assault course which is the best, or rather the hardest, in the land. It is specifically designed

This particular confidence test takes place 44 feet above the ground. However, after using the trainasium regularly in training, a recruit does not often fail on this piece of apparatus.

Long ago, a soldier died using the trainasium; his memory is always in the back of a recruit's mind during this test of confidence, agility and sheer guts.

to test to the maximum. Each obstacle is strategically placed to be of optimum difficulty and to ensure that a recruit cannot get a rhythm. The wet and muddy course must be completed not once but three times in under seven and a half minutes in order to pass. Exhausting though it is, the recruits receive vociferous encouragement round the course from the staff and fellow participants and this undoubtedly helps psychologically even if it cannot aid the physical endeavour required to beat the clock.

Despite immense fatigue, that evening the recruits must pack their bergens (rucksacks) for the next stage of the test week which takes place in Brecon, South Wales.

In winter, ice on the muddy water jumps has to be broken as the recruits attempt the assault course.

This assault course is known as the toughest in the land. It was devised so that contestants would have no chance of developing a rhythm.

DAY 3: Admittedly, it is not as fast as the ten-miler of the previous day but the eighteen-mile approach march is completed at a very quick pace nonetheless and recruits are still carrying 35lb bergens and 7lb weapons. A steep hill at the start of the event sets a painful tone for the rest of the tab. This is followed by a steady, gruelling climb and then once on to the flatter sections of the route, the pace is stepped up with long bouts of doubling. This event is extremely tiring and demands determination, stamina and endurance. If the recruits have not

The march over Fan Fawr takes place only minutes after the recruits finish climbing Pen-y-fan, the second highest mountain in South Wales. Both ascents are gruelling: Pen-y-fan is sharp and aggressively steep, while Fan Fawr is a long, protracted drag up to the top and psychologically wearing.

already suffered foot problems, it is likely that their feet will need medical attention after this punishing march.

The cure for blisters and bergen burns (where the bergen rubs the back raw) is almost worse than the ailment itself. Often on the side of the road rather than in the medical centre, the medics will slice open a man's blisters and pour on tint benz. It is agonising but it is the only way of toughening the feet so that the recruit can continue. Other members of the platoon often watch this 'treatment' to see how bravely the patient reacts.

The fledgling soldiers learn basic soldiering skills in Wales after passing P Company.

Although the greatest challenge is behind them, soldiers can still be sent back for further training if they don't make the grade on Basic Wales.

DAY 4: In the morning, the towering face of the highest mountain in South Wales awaits the exhausted recruits. Pen-y-fan is a very steep, long climb and virtually demands rock climbing to reach the final peak which is frequently covered in ice during the winter months. After a short respite at the windswept top, a rapid descent awaits, which is guaranteed to cripple the knees, especially when carrying heavy weight.

After a brief rest for lunch and a change of socks, the recruits tackle Fan Fawr. This is not as steep or high as Pen-y-fan but it is a long and demoralisingly visible haul up and down at a smart pace and is particularly tough so soon after the other ascent. Those who struggled to complete Pen-y-fan will almost certainly fail to finish Fan Fawr.

Psychologically, the afternoon's event is probably the toughest of the week. It is a speed march and after two days of tabbing in the mountains, it is dreaded by the recruits. It covers a ten-kilometre route through narrow winding lanes, which must be completed in under one hour ten minutes to score maximum points. As with all events, there is a psychological line five metres behind the main body to which recruits drop back as they tire. Ironically, they often maintain their position at this point with the main body always tantalisingly in sight ahead but they are simply unable to make up the gap. A few may manage to beat the clock even from the five-metre line but there will always be those who cannot sustain the effort and give up or who are taken out. Staff will encourage a recruit on the event as much as possible but once they decide that he cannot succeed, they will order him to stop. Recruits often resist, insisting they can make it, but there can be no argument. They are forced to follow their companions in the back of a Land Rover before being returned to Depot.

Very often during the winter months, the top of Pen-y-fan is covered in ice; conditions are treacherous and possibly deadly.

DAY 5:   By the final day, after an often cold and miserable night sleeping outdoors in a copse at the base of Pen-y-fan, every remaining man is exhausted and the smallest effort hurts a great deal. The theory of changeover techniques for the stretcher race is practised the previous evening but nothing except sheer determination will get them through this final event. The 150lb steel stretcher is carried over seven and a half miles of road by a rotational team of an optimum of twelve. Four carry the stretcher, four carry the stretcher-bearers' weapons, and four wait to take over the stretcher. This is the ideal scenario but numbers are dictated by how many are left on the course. There is a steep hill towards the end of the route and whichever team reaches it first usually wins the race. It is a painful and punishing experience for everyone, irrespective of placings, and it takes sheer guts to get through it, particularly if any members of your team drop out. Completion of the course is not a guarantee of success since this event is against the clock and every recruit's individual input to the event is gauged. Even though it is a set test, if the officer commanding P Company decides that the teams were not trying hard enough, it is not unknown for a further one and a half miles to be added to the route.

The fact that a recruit has completed every event and is still on P Company does not necessarily mean that he has passed. For some, the points they have scored throughout P Company test week are not enough to secure success and they must return to Aldershot for further training and another try at the P Company ordeal at a later date. Some fail on attitude. Of the full platoon that started thirteen weeks previously, only 25 to 33 per cent will earn their red berets at this first attempt.

Throughout the test week, recruits are chivvied and vocally harangued by staff who are striving to get the best performance from each individual. There is a great deal of robust physical

The stretcher race is the last event and particularly tough. It takes team effort to do well, yet each recruit is judged individually.

encouragement during test events in the form of dragging, pushing and the occasional well-aimed slap on the back of the helmet. The vast majority of recruits said that they accepted this rough treatment as a necessary evil in order to pass P Company. Far from being resented, the seemingly harsh assistance meted out by staff was considered almost essential for success and few felt that they could pass simply on their own motivation.

While recruits change and prepare for parade, P Company staff immediately go into consultation to determine who has passed. Each recruit's scores are carefully checked and if there are any borderline cases, reports on their performance are given by the PPS sergeant. P Company staff have no opportunity to get to know individuals on a recruit PPS and they therefore judge each man purely on results and his performance on the day. Once decisions have been made by P Company staff, the

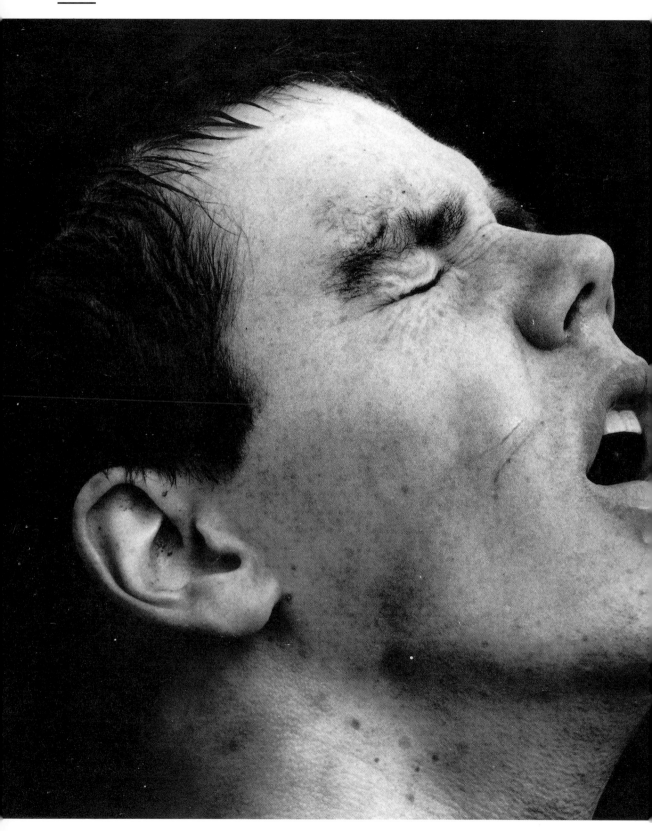

Sheer exhaustion mixed with relief at having completed yet another event.

Even the toughest need to sleep. Paras soon learn the art of getting some 'head down', but for the recruits it's usually sheer exhaustion.

platoon staff who have worked with these men for thirteen weeks are invited in and the decisions plus a brief report on each individual are announced. It is very rare that the platoon staff receive any surprises or unexpected disappointments. However, if there has been an uncharacteristically poor performance by an individual, platoon staff will vouch for his character and, if he is a borderline case, his result will be discussed further, but P Company staff have the final say on who passes and who fails. There is no room for compassion in this decision process since the staff know that their lives may one day be entrusted to successful recruits. The standard for success must be high and consistent. There is no set quota of passes to achieve. Staff believe that if a recruit is made of the right calibre material, he will be sufficiently determined to put himself through the ordeal again in order to win his red beret.

The recruits are formed up and the officer commanding (OC) P Company reads out the names and results. Those who have failed are marched away to return for retraining if they have the mental and physical courage. For the remaining men, the proudest moment of all has arrived – the presentation of their red berets. It is an intensely emotional moment, a mixture of relief, joy and pride. As they remove their forage caps and put on the coveted red beret, these exhausted men physically straighten and grow a few inches. After the presentation, the OC tells the successful recruits to 'wear your beret with pride – you've earned it'. They have also earned a well-deserved night of celebration on the town for which they always manage to find just enough energy.

ALL ARMS The All Arms volunteers, established soldiers of all ranks from units supplying troops to 5 Airborne Brigade, must pass the same gruelling P Company test but obviously the preparation differs slightly. It is allegedly possible to pass P

Company with sufficient individual training but it requires huge self-discipline and dedication and the vast majority of passes are gained by those who attend a Pre-PPS course at one of the units that send a steady stream of volunteers. Courses run by 7 Para Royal Horse Artillery (7RHA), 148 Battery Royal Artillery (RA), 9 Para Squadron Royal Engineers (RE), Signals Squadron and the Logistical Battalion of 5 Airborne Brigade are all specifically designed to prepare men in the three or four weeks prior to P Company. The courses are run for their own personnel and for others from their corps.

For the All Arms PPS, which also comprises Parachute Regiment officers, the P Company course consists of two weeks of intensive physical build-up followed by the test week outlined above. Throughout the three weeks, men will return to their units due to injury or because they do not make the grade. P Company staff have an opportunity to get to know individuals over this longer period, something they cannot do with the recruits, and so they are able to judge characters for themselves as well as making sure individuals achieve the required physical standard. For the P Company staff, it is a rare opportunity to have officers at their mercy, so to speak, and most officers emerging successfully from P Company would admit that it is a character-forming experience. PPS staff readily admit that the Parachute Regiment officers are given the hardest ride of all and that staff are particularly tough with them since they expect the highest possible standards from their own men. More than any others, Parachute Regiment officers must excel.

P Company deliberately pushes men to their extreme of fitness and then starts testing them. Physical effort at this level is a measure more of a candidate's willpower and determination than of fitness. Any volunteer must be prepared to work continually to his limits and beyond and must never stop giving maximum effort. Lack of courage or tenacity is considered a

The proudest moment of
all is when the recruits
replace their forage
caps with the coveted
red beret.

Berets are a uniform
shape when presented.
The men soak them in
water and mould them
to their own particular
style. There is a
surprising amount of
variation and
individuality in the
finished results.

greater weakness than being physically unable to complete the task. Obviously, the fitter a candidate is on arrival, the better he is able to cope with the stresses of the course and the greater his chance of avoiding injuries; in 25 per cent of cases where men are returned to their units from All Arms PPS, it is because of injury. Only after successfully completing the three-week course culminating in P Company test week will the red beret be presented. Similarly, there is no quota system and All Arms men pass purely on merit against a consistent standard, so passing numbers vary a great deal. As with the recruits, it is a moment of great pride and heightened self-confidence. All Arms candidates then have the option of continuing at a later date to Brize Norton for parachute selection, while Parachute Regiment officers go there directly.

ADVANCED WALES Parachute Regiment recruits stay in Brecon for three weeks after P Company to complete their training so that they can take their place as a Grade 3 Rifleman in a rifle section of a Parachute battalion. Although the ordeal of P Company is behind them, the pressure is maintained since there is a great deal to learn before they can join the battalion. They are now tested on their basic soldiering skills and recruits can still be back-squadded if they fail Advanced Wales, though this is rare.

Recruits receive an introduction to the basic techniques of surviving in the field such as constructing battle trenches and making shelters, a prerequisite of combat. They also learn defence tactics, battle drills, attack and ambush skills, helicopter drills, signals and map reading. A degree of personal survival knowledge must also be mastered.

To this end, recruits practise living off the land and learn how to provide themselves with food and adequate shelter. In the frequently adverse weather conditions of the Brecon Beacons,

Early in their careers soldiers undergo nuclear, biological and chemical (NBC) warfare training.

exposure and exhaustion are serious dangers to health which the recruits must learn to detect and treat immediately. Wet clothing (lying in a battle trench in the rain), high winds, low air temperatures, immersion in cold water (river crossings) and immobility (waiting in ambush for some hours) are all conditions which a soldier is likely to experience and he must learn to deal with them.

During this period, the recruits continue their education in the black humour of the Parachute Regiment. Long days in the field are lightened by injections of humour from the staff. These always come at unexpected times, such as in the middle of the night or at meal times. For example, when an over-zealous colour sergeant provides too much food, training will not recommence until every piece is eaten, no matter how full everyone feels. In typical Para style, this game is usually played against the clock.

After sixteen arduous weeks, the recruit has been transformed from a civilian into a trained soldier. He has been through incredible hardships and, against seemingly insurmountable odds, has succeeded in earning the coveted red beret. A trained rifleman he may be, but until a recruit has won his wings, his place in the Parachute Regiment as an airborne soldier is not assured. There is yet another test awaiting him at Brize Norton.

Finally leaving Depot to join the battalion and the ranks of seasoned soldiers is a moment of great anticipation and some trepidation for the newly qualified joes.

2
MILITARY PARACHUTING
RED ON, GREEN ON – GO!

Pathfinder Platoon regularly use a freefall parachute technique called HALO (high altitude, low opening) to insert into an area without detection ahead of the main body of men.

For the recruits of the Parachute Regiment, arriving at RAF Brize Norton for the four-week parachute training course is something of a relief after the rigours of P Company and Advanced Wales. No longer are they harangued by zealous staff and the physical demands of this course are much less arduous, although exacting in a different way. However, having so recently passed P Company and without the levelling

experience of joining a battalion, the recruits consider themselves fairly invincible at this stage; parachuting holds little fear for them and they are pretty full of themselves. Meanwhile, the All Arms parachute trainees reach Brize after varying degrees of experience with their own unit. All exhibit the relaxed attitude and confidence of seasoned soldiers of all ranks. A further dimension of the All Arms course is that it comprises non-5 Airborne troops, in particular the Marines, who attend the course for specific training purposes or simply for Adventurous Training. Whichever route is taken to reach the

Procedures for safe landings and parachute rolls are rehearsed *ad infinitum* in hangars before recruits put theory into practice.

Practising exits from a plane in a simulated fuselage. A 'penguin' checks his static line.

No. 1 Parachute Training School (1PTS), the fundamentals of parachuting and the course itself are the same for all.

The huge training hangar is furnished with an array of high-tech equipment which is used throughout the four-week period for ground training purposes. Before moving onto the equipment, training starts with standard administration work and theory. Each man is shown around the hangar, which will be his 'home' for the next four weeks, and then everyone is measured for height and weight. There is a height and weight restriction for parachuting of 6 foot 3 inches and 200lb respectively. Any man exceeding these limits could have serious difficulties when jumping fully laden, since his descent would be too fast for safety.

The course, which normally consists of sixty-four men, is split into two syndicates and then further divided into sections before being allocated instructors. The parachute jump instructors (PJIs) are members of the RAF Detachment to Airborne Forces and it is their job to ensure that the trainees are prepared for every parachuting eventuality. Very few of the trainees have parachuted before and those that have enjoyed sport parachuting have only a negligible advantage in that they have experienced exiting an aircraft. After that, all similarities between the two styles of parachuting end; in broad terms, everyone starts from the same point.

Firstly, position in the air, parachute landings and rolls are taught. These procedures are practised ad infinitum on mats in the hangar until they are second nature to the trainees. Theory sessions then cover details of the parachute itself and what will happen to them in the air. To illustrate this, harnesses (swings) suspended from wires are used which closely simulate a deployed parachute during descent. This enables the trainee to practise canopy counts. A static-line parachute takes two and a half seconds to open and four seconds before it is fully deployed. After this time he knows that he should check his canopy for correct deployment. If for any reason it has not opened or is not fully deployed, after briefly assessing the situation he should deploy his reserve chute. Steering away and general flight control of the parachute can also be practised in the swings.

The trainees are as well prepared as one can be in the event of an emergency. Not only do they rehearse emergency procedures in the swings but they are shown an emergency check where the reserve is actually pulled. Eventually, a lecture covers drills for the balloon car in preparation for the first and some say most frightening descent of all – the balloon jump.

BALLOON JUMP As the first descent of the course, the balloon jump usually takes place on Thursday of the first week after three days of theory and ground training. A hydrogen barrage balloon with a metal cage holding four trainees and a PJI slung below it is tethered to a winch vehicle. The balloon is winched up to 800 feet and then very calmly and cold-bloodedly the trainees are asked to stand at the open gate and then to step off.

It is a particularly unnerving experience. At 800 feet it is very quiet without the sound of an aircraft engine, and noises from the ground are eerily muffled. In this cold atmosphere, without the benefit of the adrenaline which normally flows during a flight and in the absence of group bravado, it takes considerable nerve and self-control to step calmly into the void. It also requires a certain faith in your equipment. Most seasoned Paras will confess that they hated their first balloon jump.

Unlike an aircraft jump where the slipstream whips the parachutist sideways, thus lessening the falling sensation, on the balloon jump you fall like a stone and it feels as though everything is coming up into your mouth. Although the chances of a malfunction are remote, there is always the danger that an inexperienced parachutist will use the wrong lines to steer away from the cable and head into it, so running the danger of collapsing his parachute. PJIs enthusiastically shout commands from the ground and serious accidents are rare.

A feeling of great relief usually floods the trainee when he lands safely. Relief is quickly succeeded by elation and a descent that took forty seconds to complete will take about forty minutes to recount, blow by blow. In many ways, it is worse for those who have to wait and watch from the ground as

The recruit's first jump
is from a basket
suspended under a
balloon. It is eerily
quiet. The recruit steps
into open space and
plummets like a stone.

1,000, 2,000, 3,000 ...
the moment of truth as
a recruit waits for the
static line to pull out
his chute.

groups of four slowly attempt the descent. If at any stage a trainee should refuse to jump, the man is given the benefit of the doubt and the command will be repeated once more in case there was some misunderstanding. If he refuses again, he is automatically removed from the course. In the case of Parachute Regiment recruits, this is effectively the end of their career. Similarly, if at any time the 1PTS staff consider a trainee not to be up to scratch or a threat to others in the air, that man will be failed. Once a trainee has refused a descent or voluntarily taken himself off the course, there is no second chance.

The balloon jump has become synonymous with a test of courage and character but it originated for more practical reasons. The high cost of aircraft time and the strong possibility of delay due to unsuitable weather conditions make aircraft descents impractical for training purposes. A balloon can be set up for an extended period at a relatively modest cost and large numbers of trainees can pass through during a short span of time.

Celebrations take place in the Spotlight Club situated in Brize Norton camp. This is the first opportunity for the Penguins, so-called because they have their berets but not their wings, to let off steam as the end of training is now in sight. The girls who come to the club have to endure countless tales of derring-do after the first balloon jump, and of course they have heard it all before.

AIRCRAFT DESCENTS The emphasis at 1PTS is on encouraging confidence rather than obeying shouted orders, and as the trainees' self-assurance grows, this approach can sometimes be misconstrued as a 'soft' touch. However, with an unusual mixture of humour and baffling superior technical knowledge, the PJIs generally manage to impress upon course members the seriousness of parachuting and the life-threatening dangers of taking the course lightly. It is always stressed that trainees take responsibility for themselves and if they endanger their own lives, that is their choice, but irresponsible behaviour must not threaten the safety of other parachutists at any time.

The next stage of training involves more simulators which include a mock-up of the interior of a Hercules aircraft, an advanced landing trainer (known as the Fan), and the outdoor exit trainer (known as the knacker-cracker). With the aid of these pieces of equipment, flight drills, landings and aircraft exits are repeatedly practised in the hangar.

Flight Drills: Inside the replica hull of the Hercules an exact re-enactment of the in-flight situation can be carried out. Trainees practise all the drills that will take place in the air, including seating formations and numbering off. From there, the first stick (line of men) goes through the motions of hooking up and hanging onto the strop. Each man checks his own equipment according to a set procedure. He also checks the man in front. Then each parachutist is in turn checked again by the PJI. In reverse order, the stick 'tells off', which means each man stating his number in the stick and calling 'OK', simultaneously hitting the shoulder of the man in front so that engine noise cannot cause confusion. If anyone is dissatisfied with his equipment, he will not 'tell off'. When all the safety procedures are completed, the whole stick moves forward with a shuffling gait known as the airborne shuffle, whereby the left leg leads and the right leg is dragged behind. This is because in an operational situation, a large, heavy container of fighting equipment is strapped to the right leg and a parachutist is obliged to drag this behind him. As they exit from the simulator, trainees are checked for a good exit position and a nice, tight position in the air, with feet and knees together for a gentle landing.

The Fan: This consists of a platform about forty feet above the ground and two wrist straps attached to chains, which are used to practise jumping off in the correct position. By moving the chains sideways, forwards or backwards, different landings can be rehearsed. The descent is gently arrested by an airbrake system.

Outdoor Exit Trainer: Again, this is a simulated aircraft hull with a door suspended about forty feet above the ground. Wires to which a trainee is attached in a tight groin harness lead down to the ground. Trainees are expected to exit as they would from an aircraft and a driving, vigorous leap is needed so that a man's momentum will carry him along the wires (simulating the movement of the slipstream) safely to the ground. If his exit is less than enthusiastic, he will tend to jerk painfully up and down on the wires – hence the equipment's quaint nickname of the knacker-cracker.

On Friday of the first week, weather permitting, the first aircraft jump will be attempted. For some, it is the first time they have been in a plane, let alone jumped out of it. Although the training has been thorough, the tense faces of the parachutists tell their own story. Bravado gives way to contemplative thought and everyone becomes very quiet. Unlike the balloon jump where the last thing anyone wants to do is step out, by the time the trainees have experienced an extended period of low-level flying with a number of them making full use of the sick bags provided, the majority are actually keen to get out of the aircraft. After running through the familiar security checks, the first single stick of six men wait for the green light. With two minutes to go, the PJI opens up the side parachute door of the Hercules and the first man steps into position. This is perhaps the most tense moment as the red light comes on indicating 'Make ready' just before it changes to green for 'Go'. At that moment, action takes over from tense

Surviving the 'knacker-cracker'.

anticipation and the whole stick is dispatched in a hurried yet controlled fashion. This is where earlier training on the trainasium comes into its own because it is easy to freeze in the doorway.

As each man steps into the door, his hand is knocked away from his strop by the PJI and he is hit on the shoulder to jump out. At that moment, the range of expressions on their faces varies from sheer terror through studied concentration to wild excitement. After their exit, the PJIs drag the static lines back into the plane and these are removed ready for the next stick to hook up for the following pass over the drop zone (DZ).

'Exhilarating' is the general consensus of opinion after a first aircraft jump. Most people experience excitement simultaneously with fear, followed by a feeling of complete elation when they are safely on the ground. Most agree that it is far superior to the balloon jump, if only because they know what is going on. By the second jump, which is in single sticks of ten, the trainees are beginning to enjoy it and, with the proviso of 'once the chute is open', all found it a brilliant experience.

These first few training descents are called clean fatigue jumps, which means that the parachutists are jumping without any additional equipment. The trainees progress from single-stick descents to simultaneous (sim) sticks, namely exiting from both side doors of the aircraft at the same time with a split-second delay between the two sticks. It is at this stage that it is imperative for the trainees to observe their training and exit on the PJI's command. If anyone hesitates or goes too soon, he runs the risk of meeting his opposite number on the other side as the slipstream pulls him under the belly of the aircraft and this can cause entanglements and serious accidents.

The fifth jump is completed at night. There is no specific training for this although some PJIs make their groups go through the ground training with their eyes shut, and this is the last jump before they start parachuting with equipment.

It is fairly easy at this stage to overtrain, particularly if the weather is bad and the course is confined to the hangar. The course relies heavily on the personality of individual PJIs to keep morale high and spirits lifted. If the trainees cannot complete their eight qualifying jumps due to poor weather conditions, every effort is made to carry the course over until they have completed

Every face tells a story as the door is cracked open in the Hercules ready for the jump.

the statutory number of jumps, otherwise they have to return at a later date.

As with clean fatigue jumps, equipment descents are built up gradually, starting with small single sticks and culminating in a large sim stick equipment jump. The eighth, and final, qualifying jump is as near to operational as the PJIs can make it. Each man carries all his personal fighting equipment packaged in a container with a weapon sleeve and a simulated weapon plus a parachutist life preserver (PLP, or life jacket). All previous aircraft jumps are carried out at 1,000 feet, but for the operational training descent the exit height is 800 feet, which means less time for correcting any errors. There is no input from the instructors, who on all previous attempts have shouted corrections and advice from the ground. On their qualifying jump, the parachutists are on their own. Whenever possible and weather permitting, a ninth operational jump is organised onto Salisbury Plain but this is not needed to earn their wings.

Throughout the course, there is a debrief after each descent. Additionally, after the balloon jump, the first aircraft descent and the first equipment descent, an individual critique is given by the instructors covering exit, observation, steering away, etc. The senior officer at the drop zone monitors performance throughout the four-week period and if he considers that the general standard is poor in any particular area, for example landings, then the instructors will concentrate on these weaknesses during ground training in the hangar.

On completion of the final qualifying jump, sometimes even on the DZ itself, a small parade is held and the wing commander from RAF Brize Norton presents each successful member with his wings. This is the culmination of all the training. Parachute Regiment recruits are now qualified to join their battalions and All Arms members can return to their units as fully qualified airborne soldiers.

Safe landings are something to smile about. The most common injuries in military parachuting are twisted ankles and broken legs.

THE REAL THING Once at battalion, exercise parachuting is a very different ball game to training. The old hands tell the new boys exactly what they need to carry and the best ways to make the parachuting experience as comfortable and convenient as possible, but jumping into an exercise with the sky full of other parachutists is something for which nothing can prepare you.

It does not take long to acquire the Para knack of being able to fall asleep at any given opportunity and it is amazing how many men will have their heads down on the aircraft before it has even left the runway. If conditions seemed cramped at Brize Norton, they are immeasurably worse on an operational jump. The brigade uses both the Hercules Mark 1 and the Mark 3 which carry up to ninety paratroops (not including dispatchers and cabin crew). In addition to the men, on the rear ramp of the aircraft, using a platform called a wedge, two containers are carried and these are dropped onto the DZ immediately prior to the troop drop.

On most exercises, there would also be a heavy drop from non-troop-bearing aircraft, involving guns and vehicles on platforms. Smaller stores are air-dropped using containers. Naturally, as a safety precaution, this equipment is dropped onto a different DZ to that of personnel, although it is reasonably nearby.

At the start of any exercise, there are normally two to three hours of low-level flying before insertion. This is a deeply unpleasant experience; the flight is very bumpy and tends to be fairly airless. This, coupled with the extreme heat and close, semi-lit conditions in the back of the Hercules, often results in men being sick and once one starts, it tends to trigger off a chain reaction. Stomach settlers and ear protectors are handed out by the PJIs before the start of the flight but it is seldom enough to prevent some sickness, particularly if the men have been on the beer the night before, as is likely. The planes fly in at 200 feet, at which level a great deal of turbulence is experienced, and then pass up very rapidly to 800 feet for the jump.

Unlike civil flights, there is no smoking throughout the journey and the only in-flight entertainment is information on weather conditions and jump timings which is handed round by the PJIs. For the longer flights, a somewhat Heath Robinson toilet is rigged up at the back of the plane.

Every man is heavily laden with his bergen packed to survive several days on the ground, plus a weapon, parachute and reserve. The bergen alone usually weighs in the region of 110lb and this rises dramatically with the extra food, ammunition, mortars and grenades that are carried so each section has enough fire power and food to perform an operational task.

Moments after the wedge has been dispatched, troops move into the door. On an operational jump, time is limited over the DZ and so every man in the aircraft must exit as quickly as possible on the green light. If for any reason the light command system should fail, the load master gives the signals manually as he receives commands through his headset from the cockpit.

By the time they approach the DZ, everyone is keen to get out of the smelly, sticky atmosphere of the Hercules but this is not always as easy as it sounds. Moving into position in cramped conditions with extremely heavy, unwieldy equipment is no mean feat. At the door the PJIs help the parachutists out with an encouraging shove. There is only a one-second interval between the men exiting the aircraft from the two side doors. The sky is full of parachutists and this is the time when there is a very real danger of accidents. With so many canopies within a limited space, an airsteal may occur. This happens when the air that would normally inflate a canopy disappears as another

When setting off on
exercise the men are
laden with kit:
irrespective of size,
they often carry bergens
weighing in excess of
100 lb.

Drop at dawn.

parachute passes below. In this case, the upper canopy collapses. There are precautions that can be taken to avoid such incidents but the parachutists must be alert at all times to these dangers and steer away where necessary. Collisions, too, can happen when the sky is so full. Tall tales abound about parachuting incidents and every soldier has a story to tell about a close shave. It is not unknown for someone to run across the top of another man's canopy in order to get away, nor for two men to descend together under one chute after an entanglement that deflates one of their canopies.

Once a parachute is safely deployed, each man must drop his bergen which is suspended on a nylon line. Should he fail to do so for any reason, this again can lead to serious injury on landing. The rarity of serious accidents in the air and fatalities is testimony to the brigade's parachuting skill.

On the DZ, the medics and field ambulance are there to attend to any injuries that may have occurred. Twisted ankles or broken legs are common when the parachutist lands heavily. Other injuries occur when parachutists land in trees or collide with other immovable objects. Most injuries are treated on the ground but in more serious cases the helicopters are called in and the casualty is evacuated from the DZ to a nearby hospital.

Military parachuting does not always involve jumping into a field on Salisbury Plain. DZ hazards range from the Northumbrian wilds of Otterburn with its sheep sheds and potholes to built-up areas with electric pylons and buildings. Some scenarios demand parachuting onto airfields and so jumping onto concrete is sometimes rehearsed, although nothing the individual can do reduces the increased risk of high-impact injury. Parachuting from different types of aircraft including helicopters is also practised, as are water jumps where the parachutist lands in sea or open water.

Exercises are regularly organised with other countries so that

Parachute Jump Instructors (PJIs) freefall training at Brize Norton.

Paras have an opportunity to experience different styles of parachuting and to be awarded another set of wings. In France, for example, the dispatchers take a far less active role. When the time comes to exit the aircraft, a hooter sounds and everyone just rushes out the back of the plane without delay. French PJIs resort to smiling at the parachutists on their way out and saluting the officers as they rush past.

All those who wear their wings must complete four jumps a year to qualify for extra parachute pay, unless operationally committed. Ironically, many of the Parachute Regiment do not enjoy military parachuting and do it simply because it is an integral part of their job. Jumps cancelled as late as in the air are usually greeted with sarcastic moans and comments such as 'Oh, what a pity!' However, there are some who get a great deal of satisfaction from sport parachuting and, for them, there is the option of joining the freefall parachute display team, the Red Devils, or, at a more functional level, the Pathfinders unit.

Although they have other roles to fulfil, the two main objectives of the Pathfinder unit are securing and marking DZs for the main brigade (both personnel and heavy drop) and forward reconnaissance. Since Pathfinders need to be inserted ahead of the main body without detection, all members must be proficient at high altitude low opening (HALO) parachuting techniques. For this, troops exit at heights between 12,000 and 25,000 feet, from where the aircraft's engine noise cannot be heard on the ground, and then freefall to a height at which chutes can be safely opened. To enable men to fly at altitudes above 10,000 feet, the Hercules is specially equipped with oxygen units. In order to keep their small teams together, Pathfinders must also be experienced in altering their rate of descent and 'tracking' (moving sideways) across the sky.

In contrast to normal military parachuting, at 25,000 feet it is usually the tail ramp at the back of the Hercules which is opened. On the green light, everyone rushes towards the open doorway and leaps headlong into space. Pathfinders drop for about one minute fifty seconds at a speed of 120 mph. Altimeter readings are taken regularly and at about 6,000 feet the group separate slightly before the automatic opening device on the parachute pack takes effect. Once the chute is safely deployed, each man moves towards the lowest man in his patrol so that they land together. At 1,000 feet, the bergen is loosed and left to dangle from its nylon line.

On landing, the oxygen mask, helmet and goggles are removed and, on an operational jump, the parachute is hidden before continuing with the mission. On an exercise, however, it is just one more item to carry.

Needless to say, further specialist training is given in freefall parachuting on passing selection for Pathfinders and candidates are drawn from all units of 5 Airborne with a tendency towards the more experienced, older members of the brigade. They still practise standard parachuting methods but the vast majority of their work involves HALO, and a certain liking for freefall is not so much a prerequisite as a sensible preference.

3
LIFE IN BATTALION
FROM CROW TO TOM

'To meet the requirements of 5 Airborne Brigade's dual roles the soldier must be fit, tough, aggressive and mentally robust, with the self-sufficiency to operate on light scales and the flexibility to react to the unexpected; in short, the airborne soldier.'

Brigadier D.R. Chaundler OBE (Commander of 2 Para in the Falklands after Colonel H. Jones died).

High spirits at the annual Christmas party where, once a year, officers and senior NCOs wait on the men.

The everyday life of an airborne soldier is robust and demanding. It is a far cry from the nine-to-five routine of many civilians. Army life demands a total commitment and many long hours, often including weekends, and lengthy periods away from home. There can be few other professions where at every stage of its development, the job has such a direct effect on lifestyle and family. The considerable amount of time spent in the company of fellow soldiers, with many of the single, younger men living together in blocks, combined with the shared, unifying experience of P Company, produces a great camaraderie and lifelong friendships. For those who have been through battle together, such as in the Falklands, the bonds are even greater and it is true to say that, in the purest sense of the word, these men genuinely love one another.

There is a great deal of banter and joking and practical jokes are played incessantly. The unfortunate young soldier straight from Depot is bound to be the butt of many jokes and it is little comfort at the time to know that everyone else has been through the same initiation procedure. Wicked humour and lightning-quick retorts are the hallmark of the airborne soldier. The sense of humour borders on the black side but this is scarcely surprising considering their rugged and sometimes dangerous existence. Even in the bleakest moment when morale is at its lowest ebb, someone invariably comes out with a comment that makes everyone laugh and breaks the mood. If a soldier is to survive comfortably in a battalion, he must sharpen his wit to defend himself verbally. As a result, the standard of repartee is often worthy of the best cabaret circuits.

However, every member of 5 Airborne is aware that they have a serious function to perform and the honing of skills for this role is intensive. The brigade is part of the British Army's out-of-area force and maintains one battalion ready to move at any time, known as the Lead Parachute Battalion Group (LPBG).

Platoon staff swapping stories back at the office.

Their function requires light mobile forces ready to operate in any area of the world, usually inserting by air. The role demands the ability to work independently without flanking formations and with extended lines of communication and a logistic system which is tailored to cope with these specific tasks.

The out-of-area (OAA) role comprises tasks such as reinforcing dependent territories, the protected evacuation of UK nationals from potentially dangerous situations, assisting friendly governments, carrying out international peacekeeping operations and any other unexpected eventuality which requires an adaptable, highly professional, quick reaction force. Such a multifarious role requires meticulous preparation and extensive exercising.

Airborne exercises can be of diverse scales ranging from a single company of approximately one hundred men to full brigade involvement, or even as part of a NATO exercise. In any event, airborne soldiers would normally expect to be inserted by air, either by parachute or air-land assault. Naturally, every member of the two in-role parachute battalions can jump in and a percentage of all the other units of 5 Airborne are qualified to parachute. Indeed, this is a prerequisite for all members of the LPBG. However, the majority of the brigade are trained in air-landing assaults which could be by means of Hercules aircraft or various types of helicopter.

5 AIRBORNE BRIGADE BATTLE ORDER

(ORBAT) The 5,500-strong brigade is totally autonomous and, although large, it is a lightly equipped formation which is ideal for its airborne role. The four infantry battalions usually include two Parachute battalions, a Gurkha battalion and one standard infantry battalion who are based in Canterbury and fulfil this function on a short-term, rotational basis. All are trained in air landing from Hercules, if not parachuting.

Meanwhile, Life Guards, 7 Royal Horse Artillery (RHA), 36 Engineer Regiment (incorporating 9 Para Squadron), one Signal Squadron, the Pathfinder Platoon and Explosive Ordnance Device (EOD) Troop all have specialist knowledge and accordingly perform their specific functions once they have parachuted or been air-landed into position. Their essential equipment such as the 105mm light guns of the Artillery is airportable, heliportable or can be parachuted on a medium stressed platform.

In addition, the Logistics Battalion which forms the support and supply branch of the brigade comprises 63 Squadron Royal Corps of Transport (RCT), 82 Ordnance Company and 10 Field Workshop Royal Electrical and Mechanical Engineers (REME). Their specific function is to provide a second line to the brigade and to resupply them for up to seven days. After this, further supplies are provided through a brigade maintenance area (BMA) set up by Logistics normally at the airhead (an airfield or port which has been secured in an earlier operation). The arrival of third line support through the airhead and the BMA allows the brigade to be self-sufficient for a period of thirty days. Further support for extended overseas operations would probably follow by sea.

On the ground, the Combat Supplies Battalion (part of Logistics) have direct responsibility for supplying airborne soldiers with rations, fuel, ammunition and anything else that has been dropped in and is needed. They also supply a helicopter handling team who take charge of loading and unloading underslung nets etc. If it is an on-going operation, they mark the drop zones for further supplies and clear them for when they are required by the brigade.

The REME workshop provides a recovery and repair facility for the brigade and they deal with all front-line mechanical and electrical equipment. They also provide a one-ton Land Rover with a crane attached for removal of damaged vehicles and so forth.

Finally, and of vital importance, is the 23 Parachute Field Ambulance (medical personnel) and 160 Company RMP (military police) who form the remainder of the support element of 5 Airborne Brigade.

Since the brigade is normally inserted by air, to be totally autonomous it requires its own aircraft, helicopters, pilots, crew and ground crew. To this end, 658 Aviation Squadron AAC (Army Air Corps) and two Tactical Air Control Parties make up the final element of 5 Airborne Brigade. Additionally, the RAF supports the brigade with a fleet of sixty-one Hercules and guarantees to provide twenty-one aircraft within seventy-two hours to enable the LPBG to deploy. The RAF also maintains tactically trained crews to fly the aircraft in this role. Support helicopters (SH) are also available to the brigade on deployment. They would reach the area of operations either by flying direct, by carriage on a Hercules, or by sea.

This comprehensive and multifaceted group is presided over and co-ordinated by Brigade Headquarters, Intelligence and the Air Force Liaison Section (AFLS).

ON EXERCISE During any exercise, irrespective of size, there is a great deal of waiting around interspersed with bursts of frantic activity. The wartime adage of 'hurry up and wait' holds true to this day. Mounting an airborne exercise requires a great deal of preparation and the best-laid plans remain at the mercy of the weather. Adverse conditions can mean the departure time for the exercise is delayed and high winds often result in last-minute changes to plans so that troops are air-landed instead of parachuted in. However, standard procedures must be carried out to the original time schedule in case timings go to plan.

A Paratrooper fires a Browning machine gun.

Everyone gathers in the huge, vaulted hangars at the departure airfield and the jumping order is established for each aircraft. Men who will be working closely together on the ground are divided between the aircraft so that they can be dropped in roughly the same place. Similarly, key officers are spread between the aircraft for obvious safety reasons. Once the jumping order has been established, the seating arrangements of the Hercules are simulated in the hangar by chalked lines on the ground and each man is given his number in the stick. Dummy runs are practised time and time again until the procedure is second nature.

Despite an invariably early rise, the flight is frequently delayed for some hours. To pass the time, impromptu games of football are organised in the empty hangars as a means of dispelling pent-up energy. This often turns into a variation of the game which has no rules and, with good reason, is called murder ball. Otherwise, there is a lot of sitting in empty hangars or sipping tea in the NAAFI.

Hurry up and wait. The men while away the hours, their equipment laid out ready, as they wait for the instruction to load onto the planes.

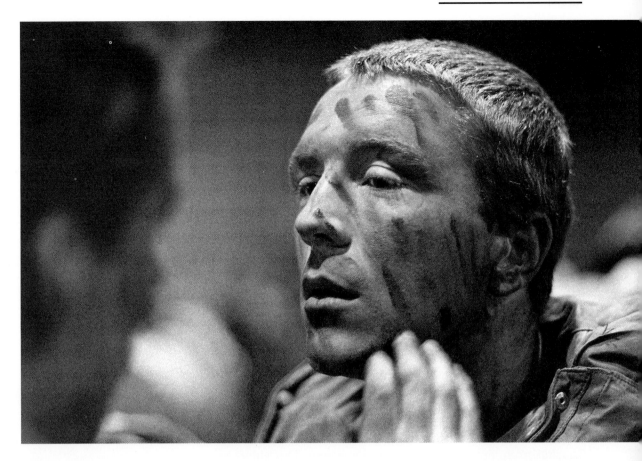

Men prepare carefully with camouflage cream before a night exercise.

When the departure time is finally confirmed, the atmosphere changes completely. Once again, parachutes and bergens are safety checked along the chalk sticks. After loading up with their heavy kit, soldiers make their way slowly to the waiting aircraft and take their places in the cramped, semi-lit interior. Many men are settled down and asleep before the plane has even left the runway. No one looks forward to several hours of low-level flying which causes faint nausea at best and severe air sickness at worst. Conversation is hampered by the noise but, in any event, most men prefer to sleep or sit quietly with their own thoughts.

Trying to manoeuvre a heavy bergen of 110lb and more plus a parachute, a reserve and a weapon through a confined aisle is not an easy task. Those in specialist platoons will have the additional burden of possibly mortar base-plates, tubes, machine-gun tripods, heavy radios and extra ammunition to bear. Many of these men in particular need assistance to move in and out of the aircraft. On the green light, there is organised, frenetic activity as men are dispatched through both side doors of the plane. It is an impressive sight as the sky fills with canopies, and time seems suspended as parachutists float silently to the ground.

On the DZ, men gather up their chutes and make their way to the rendezvous point. If it is a hot DZ, which means that enemy forces are there when the soldiers land, the attack commences straightaway. Casualties in the form of twisted or broken ankles and legs due to a rough landing are quickly located and treated by the medics. If the injury is serious, they may be flown to hospital by helicopter or removed by Land Rover.

Attacks on an objective are mounted quickly, quietly and efficiently. These invariably involve tabbing over a considerable distance in a short time since for obvious reasons the parachutists do not land too close to the enemy. This ability to move quickly with weight was ably demonstrated in the Falklands conflict. A pre-arranged formula for the attack will be mounted. After the objective is achieved, prisoners taken or evacuees rescued, depending on the scenario, each section makes its way to the appointed rendezvous.

Meanwhile, a headquarters is set up elsewhere and an operations (Ops) room established where the next stage of the exercise is planned. The HQ is also a communication centre and all information from the field is filtered through it. Although there is a great deal happening at all times, in the main those officers involved tend to remain calm and unflustered despite the pressure. Conversation is terse and to the point. From information gathered from those on the ground, the commanding officer amends and updates his plan and

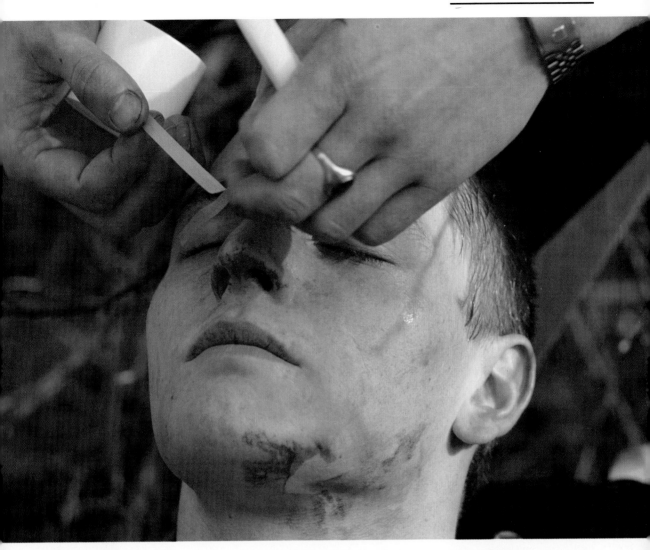

Injuries while on exercise are treated in the field by the medics.

discusses ideas with his senior officers. Suggestions are put forward and possible flaws discussed. When the plan is finalised, the finer details and timings are worked out and the information is then disseminated to other ranks in the field.

An important part of the detailed information fed to the Ops room is provided by the Pathfinder platoon. They would have freefallen into the area in advance of the main body of the brigade and secured and marked the personnel and stores DZs. They allow themselves only the minimum amount of time

Snipers can wreak such damage on an enemy that they know that, in wartime, they are unlikely ever to be allowed to surrender alive.

needed to do the task and no longer, since the chances of compromise are high and surprise is one of the major advantages of an airborne assault.

Once the brigade assault has been made, Pathfinders adopt a reconnaissance role up to thirty kilometres ahead of the brigade. In this role, they may be called upon for close target reconnaissance, bridge and minefield recces. Each four-man patrol comprises a commander (usually an NCO), someone responsible for demolition although not an expert, a medic and

a radio operator. They report back to the Pathfinder HQ which includes two Royal Signal NCOs who then signal the information back to brigade HQ. Advanced communications equipment is used which allows Pathfinders to communicate with the commanding officer even as he approaches the area in the Hercules. Pathfinders also have Royal Engineer representatives who can do vital engineering recces for bridges and so on.

If necessary, Pathfinders can adopt a more aggressive role including ambush, raids, equipment snatches and minor demolition. Indeed, their versatility and adaptability is immense. Because of the importance of their role, the Pathfinder Platoon, which has its own vigorous selection process, tends to attract the more experienced men from the brigade and it offers them additional skills. Their standard operating procedures prepare men well for Special Forces selection and many then move on to this option after serving some time with Pathfinders.

After the initial frantic activity, the troops start to settle in at their appointed rendezvous. At the first available opportunity, someone will light up a hexy stove and get a brew going. Airborne soldiers are especially ingenious at hiding the flame from view and all manner of inventive methods are used such as digging holes or creating shields round Land Rover wheels. A large metal mug with masking tape on the drinking lip to avoid burns is filled to the brim with either tea or hot chocolate and this is shared between the men and officers. It has an amazingly uplifting effect on morale and warms the whole body. As soon as one brew is finished, someone else will ransack their rations and start another. When possible, half an hour's sleep is grabbed wherever it can be found – and airborne soldiers can sleep in the most unlikely places.

If the exercise is to last several days, soldiers will dig trenches

Live firing at the range during Pathfinder Platoon training.

in which they live and occasionally sleep. If, however, the duration of the exercise is only two or three days, it is more likely that they will operate throughout this time without sleep or just catching a couple of hours when they can. Sleep deprivation is something that airborne soldiers must learn to accept and familiarity with this debilitating state means that they are better able to function than most in the absence of rest.

The issue of Goretex (a breathable, water-resistant material) clothing and bivvy bags has revolutionised an airborne soldier's life. Spending weeks in the field in inclement weather is no longer as miserable an experience as it used to be. Admittedly, it is still a hardship and far from comfortable but Goretex allows a soldier to stay fairly dry and therefore warm throughout the exercise, enabling him to function more efficiently. Most soldiers are quite content to crawl into their bivvy bags, pull the string of the hood tight and bed down regardless of anything the weather may hurl at them.

Each man is psyched up for a successful conquering of the enemy position and the physically demanding action of the attack itself is a great release for this contained energy. The object of an exercise might be to infiltrate behind enemy lines, take out a defensive position, attack the HQ, causing as much confusion as possible, and then quickly and quietly steal away into the night. This may entail crossing rivers, climbing fences and other obstacles and always with the utmost care to avoid detection. To complete such an exercise successfully gives every man a huge surge of satisfaction and a high that only the effective use of adrenaline can bring. On occasions, particularly on NATO exercises where organisation is on an immense scale, confusion can arise and there are the ensuing disappointments. During an exercise in Germany with 2 Para, after an infiltration of the sort described above, it was discovered that the enemy had already evacuated – two hours before the deadline. The

On exercise, periods of waiting are punctuated with moments of explosive action.

great sense of anti-climax after such effort was obvious and each man returned in dejected spirits to the rendezvous. Without a focus for their accumulated adrenaline, everyone felt frustrated. Fortunately, this frustration was released with extra vigour during the attack on an unsuspecting enemy the following day. Whatever the circumstances, an ambush or attack is always completed with great enthusiasm and real aggression.

On rare occasions, families of the men are roped in to play

A helicopter evacuating 'hostages' from Salisbury Plain. Occasionally families are invited to play hostages on exercise so that they have an opportunity to see what their husbands and fathers do at work.

British evacuees and this helps to give wives a better idea of what their husbands do at work. It also gives them a fairly sleepless night. In most cases, however, WRAC personnel or other units play the parts of hostages or enemy.

Before these large-scale airborne exercises can be mounted, each soldier must be familiar with the tactics that will be used. The procedures have to be thoroughly rehearsed and there are a large number of basic training exercises with the express purpose of practising a specific aim. Every imaginable skill is incorporated and rehearsed from the basics of digging a battle trench to laying a mine. As with most things, it is practice that is the key to mastery, and skills that were learned during a recruit's days at Depot are used and honed regularly in battalion. There are drills for most eventualities covering assaults by aircraft, helicopter and boat attacks, ambushes, defence routines and withdrawal, vehicle moves, harbour drills and patrolling. Each man must be familiar with radio communication procedures, signal skills, map reading and individual navigation so that he can operate to full effect in the field. Soldiers must also be prepared for nuclear, biological and chemical warfare (NBC) and undergo exercises wearing NBC clothing and respirators which are particularly debilitating if worn for long periods due to the cumulative effect of lack of oxygen.

Textbook lessons are always given to impart the fundamentals of each skill. Yet it is the senior Toms in the battalion who give the younger soldiers the more useful, practical hints and tips on how to make the best of standard procedures on an individual level. Through years of experience in the field, they know the most time-saving and energy-effective ways to operate, the essential kit to pack and how to make life more comfortable for themselves. These are the tricks of the trade that can never be learned from a book.

BACK AT BASE The men spend a large part of their working lives away on exercise or on tour and being married to an airborne soldier invariably means that you are not going to see a great deal of your husband. If you look at the schedule of commitments for the past year for any of the units in 5 Airborne, the number of working days away from base is far in excess of that of most other regiments. This means that many men miss the special moments of family life, such as a child's first steps and words or important birthdays, not to mention the simple fact that partners miss each other. Communication is often infrequent when husbands are away on exercise or on remote, overseas tours. Most wives admit that they knew their husbands would be away a lot before they married them but that they were not prepared for just how much. One corporal's wife said, 'As a young wife, you feel very alone and you haven't got the children to help you make contact with other young mums.'

Irrespective of their husband's rank, all wives agreed that you never get used to the long periods of separation but that you learn to accept it. It is universally acknowledged that army wives everywhere hate evenings and Sundays – the times when they are alone or have to cope single-handedly with children. The longest duration of tour without wives and families is, in theory, six months. During that time, many of the wives return to their parents or friends for the occasional week in order to break up the separation time but those who have children in school are restricted by term times and it becomes far more difficult to travel. Although they miss their husbands desperately, the wives make a life for themselves in their absence and there is usually a difficult transition period when the men return and the wives' schedules and independent lifestyles face upheaval again.

Perhaps the biggest frustration for husbands and wives alike is the uncertainty army life enforces on their private lives. Because of the sheer size of the organisation, it is impossible for an individual to plan in advance because he simply does not know what might happen in the interim. Consequently, when a couple are invited to the wedding of a close friend in six months' time, for example, they cannot reply with any certainty. Even right up to the last minute there is always the risk that something unforeseen will arise and the soldier will be called away. Most families adjust to this and learn not to commit themselves but not many are adept at dispelling the disappointment of a last-minute change of plans. Friends who are not connected to the army certainly cannot understand this uncertainty.

While the men are away, their wives and families usually stay in a tightknit community largely because they tend to live as a group on army housing estates. All married personnel, irrespective of rank, are entitled to quarters. The size of abode and how long you wait is determined by a points system

On accompanied tours of Northern Ireland, families are housed on estates within the boundaries of the camp.

calculated according to size of family, length of service, previous periods of separation, rank, etc. Obviously, availability is also affected by demand in that area. Rates of payment for army accommodation are calculated on a scale loosely comparable to council housing rents. The rate for each rank is the same wherever the serviceman may live in the country, but the standard of accommodation varies widely. On many of the older sites, housing is often in a poor state of repair and in need of modernisation. Families are now encouraged to decorate their quarters, which was hitherto discouraged. Because of the regularity of house moves in army life, structural alterations are restricted and DIY additions forbidden.

The army housing estates accommodate more than just one regiment, which means that when husbands are away on tours, neighbours from another unit are able to keep an eye on solitary wives and families. There is an unspoken understanding among families that they can rely on each other, which is generally much appreciated.

Moving the family regularly is an accepted part of army life, although the rather Dickensian practice of 'marching out' is universally hated by wives. When you leave your home, a warden and the Accommodation Service Accountant (ASA) go over the house with a fine-tooth comb. This includes checking everywhere from inside the cooker to under the carpets and testing every doorbell, light switch and lock. The inspectors fill in a form with comments on each room and anything that is damaged or not up to scratch must be paid for. This rather humiliating procedure of inspection is obviously intended to safeguard incoming families and it is a necessary evil. Nonetheless, it seems that the smoothness and agreeableness of the handover depend largely on the temperament of the warden/ASA and some are extremely officious.

One of the unavoidable drawbacks of the married quarters

Wives and families are encouraged to become involved in army life as much as possible and regular events are held for their benefit.

system is that many of the younger men who marry cannot consider the option of buying their own homes and by the time they are on the more lucrative salary of a sergeant, for example, they already have a family. It is understandably difficult to step onto the property ladder when a three-bedroomed family house is required. In answer to this problem, the MoD are promoting a Buy-Let and Settle scheme. It identifies ways to allow a serviceman to purchase his own house but at the same time allows him to follow the army's preferred policy of accompanied service whenever possible. Reputable firms offer a house purchase scheme and also provide a letting service so that when a soldier leaves the army, he is already established in the property market. This scheme is still in its relative infancy and its popularity and success cannot yet be gauged.

To help young married couples in army quarters, there is also a rental system through which all essentials such as bedding, crockery and cutlery as well as furniture are available. This very often helps at the start of a marriage and items can then slowly be bought as funds become more readily available. Quarters are offered either as furnished, semi-furnished or unfurnished, depending on individual family requirements.

In terms of schooling, parents are faced with the same difficulties of choice as those in the civilian world. When based in Britain, most army children attend the local state school but because of its proximity to army housing estates, the classes consist almost exclusively of army personnel's children and inevitably there is only limited mixing with civilian children. All ranks are entitled to a boarding school allowance for their children. This is to promote continuity of education since state education is often disrupted due to the numerous moves inherent in military life. Parents have to pay a minimum of ten per cent of the school fees and this figure can sometimes be higher. If serving abroad, children's holiday flights to rejoin their parents are paid for by the army three times a year.

While all these domestic arrangements need attention, the Toms are still expected to fulfil a heavy work schedule when back at Aldershot. One of the most important soldiering skills is that of accurately firing a weapon. The majority of soldiers in 5 Airborne have SA80 rifles as their personal weapon and there is an annual personal weapon test (APWT) to ensure that each man is capable of firing to the required standard. A percentage of men within a platoon will carry light support weapons (LSWs). These are machine-guns which have a longer range than the SA80 and so are used to cover the approaches and movement of troops towards a target. Both are magazine fed and have an automatic capacity.

In a live firing exercise, attacks are studiously practised in varying numbers with the risks obviously multiplying as the number of firing men advancing toward a position increases. Safety procedures are stringent and penalties for improper use or negligent discharge (firing accidentally) are extremely high – somewhere in the region of a month's salary, regardless of rank. Laser equipment has now been developed whereby every soldier and every item of equipment can be fitted with a device that gives off a signal when the soldier is supposedly hit by a bullet. It is an effective, and safe, training device and is in great demand but it is rarely available. Most soldiers agree, however, that they are far more alert and work much harder on a live firing exercise because there is an element of risk. There is nothing that can simulate bullets hitting earth when firing at a dug-in position and nothing like live firing to bring home the dangers involved in armed conflict. Few men would deny that they get a great buzz from live firing exercises.

For those who are good shots, there is the opportunity for selection as a sniper. Each company has four snipers and they always work in pairs – one pair spotting and the other pair firing. Snipers use the Accuracy International rifle which is a 7.76 calibre, single action (one shot) weapon as compared with the 5.56 calibre of the SA80 or LSW. They get the best ammunition, which is graded to ensure more consistency between rounds, and are able to hit a head shot at 300 metres and give harassing fire at 600 metres. Selection training takes place within the battalion every six months and existing snipers are tested at similar intervals to maintain standards. A sniper must be able to fire from all positions but the favoured posture is the Hawkins position where the rear of the rifle is dug into the ground and the arm is over the butt, since this is the lowest prone position possible. However, it is not shooting accuracy that is the hardest part of a sniper's job. Being able to cover ground without being seen and remaining undetected even

Sergeant Lenny Carver goes on his morning run discussing the day to come with his Platoon Commander.

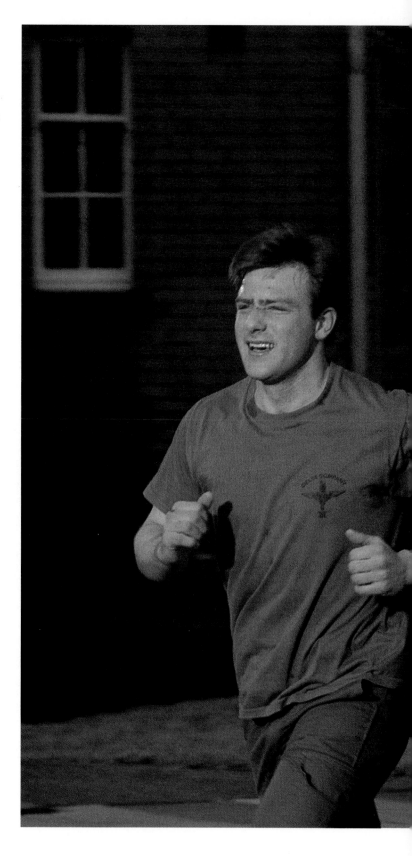

after firing is the difficulty. Because of the damage they can inflict, snipers are very dangerous and in a conflict situation they are aware that if detected, it is unlikely that they will be given an opportunity to surrender. The battalion is always reminded of the effectiveness of the Argentinian snipers 'down South' – the Falklands.

Ironically, there is not a great deal of time for target or live firing practice because the brigade has so many commitments and such an exacting schedule. Apart from numerous exercises, there are also exchange visits to other countries. This is an

Competitive sport is an important part of battalion life. There are regular inter-unit championships which are keenly contested with a great deal of rivalry between battalions and units; boxing is particularly popular among the airborne soldiers.

The Brigadier of 5 Airborne Brigade presents a medal to the winner.

opportunity for the men to earn their wings from another country and to examine at close hand the techniques employed by foreign airborne forces. Regular destinations are France, Germany, Canada, the United States, Kenya and Scandinavia. Far from being a relaxing break, these exchange trips are often hard work for the men, with tough exercises to prove the British airborne soldier's high calibre. Naturally, there are a few free days but these are generally hard-earned. The men always feel they deserve longer.

The other mainstay of activity while back in camp is fitness training and sport. As mentioned in Chapter One, men rarely maintain the peak of fitness that they achieved for P Company. However, being fit is a prerequisite of the airborne soldier's job and so there are regular sessions in the gym for circuit and weight training and frequent runs both with and without weight. Constant exercising with weight also builds stamina and endurance and the men exhibit remarkable powers of recovery after exertion. In addition to organised training, most men take it upon themselves to run in their own time and many take advantage of the weights facilities on the camp. Wednesday afternoon is set aside for sport and this tends to be team events such as soccer, rugby, hockey or basketball. Swimming is also offered and there is an army swimming test that every soldier must pass but, in broad terms, swimming ability is not high on their list of fitness priorities. Boxing is a popular pastime among the men and competition between the major units of the brigade is fierce. Regimental pride and a naturally competitive spirit mean that any contest, whether in the ring or on the pitch, is fought with enthusiasm and what is best termed as robust, high spirits. Airborne forces generally do very well in army-wide competition with the Parachute Regiment particularly noted for their cross-country running, 7RHA for their rugby and 9 Squadron for boxing.

Soldiers are entitled to two cans of beer each at the Christmas lunch, although it has been known for celebrations to continue on into the next day.

WORK HARD, PLAY HARD All ranks have a healthy social life ranging from the formal mess dinner to the raucous booze-up 'down the town'. Dinners and functions are regularly organised. Wives and girlfriends are invited to some of them; others are strictly male-only affairs. The very formal dinners are glittering occasions where ceremonial dress is worn by the men and elegant evening wear by the women, and the full regimental silver is on display. Traditions are observed and there is an unspoken code of conduct that must be followed. However, in the officers' mess at least, behaviour becomes less formal and more lively as the senior ranks depart and the subalterns are left alone to let off steam. Often the officers' mess will invite members of the senior NCOs' mess and their wives to a dinner and the compliment is then reciprocated. The meals are lengthy and the culinary standards achieved by the airborne chefs impressive.

Despite complaints, being married to an airborne soldier has its compensations and there are those who say that they gained not only a husband but a whole airborne family. Certainly a wife becomes part of a closeknit community when she shares the 'maroon' common denominator. When the battalion or squadron is back in camp, the wives attend quite a few of the social functions. In this way, spouses get to know others who live in the same area and friendships generally flourish. There are some women who feel pressured into attending functions and they resent the intrusion into their private lives. Others take the view that just because their husbands do the same job, that does not necessarily mean that the wives will have anything else in common. However, in the main, army wives appear to enjoy getting together at functions and it is usually a good opportunity for friends and workmates to relax in a more gentle and feminine atmosphere.

Social occasions serve several purposes. Obviously

Officers and men alike let their hair down with great enthusiasm during rare moments of leisure.

entertainment is a priority and, considering how hard the men work, some social reward seems well-deserved. In addition, it helps the wives to get to know each other so that when the battalion is away, it is easier for them to approach one another socially. Most of the wives said it helps to have others around them who understand their situation and that it is beneficial to share problems with other army wives who are automatically sympathetic because they have been through similar experiences. A few find this insular society too claustrophobic, particularly if they also live in army accommodation and are therefore immersed in the military twenty-four hours a day. But in general the atmosphere in the community is one of mutual support and friendship. Moreover, it is rumoured that many a warrant officer will ring his wife for an accurate update on a given situation since the wives' communication network is the best and quickest way to establish what is going on.

However, it is only recently that the army has recognised the fact that women are no longer content blindly to follow their husbands' army careers, nor are they prepared silently to endure the separations and disruptions of this lifestyle. As increasingly more men leave the forces due to family pressures, the policy-makers are beginning to pay some attention to the sensitive problem of dissatisfied wives. Although it is accepted that military duties must come first, greater efforts are being made to accommodate wives more readily in diverse ways. The opinion of the Federation of Army Wives is now regularly sought and the Federation is often consulted, for example regarding the facilities of new buildings. The Family Officers are organising open days and socials for wives, and occasionally they and the children can attempt weekend assault courses and mock exercises to give them a better idea of what their husbands' jobs involve. Similarly, coffee mornings and other events are organised and there are thriving social clubs.

Joe, the Carvers' younger son, tries his dad's helmet for size.

Organised social events apart, drinking with mates in familiar pubs in the town is a cherished and vehemently defended tradition. Aldershot is considered their town and there are certain bars, namely The Fives, The Rat Pit, The Exchange, The Trafalgar and The George, that are felt to be exclusively for Parachute Regiment and airborne forces, and others use these bars at their peril. Unwinding together over a few drinks is an integral part of airborne life. Undoubtedly there will be the familiar chuntering about poor pay and excessive hard work, as well as the usual discussions of other members of the unit, but despite these grievances, the majority of men are extremely reluctant to leave the closeknit community of airborne forces. The intense camaraderie is never more apparent than when the men are off-duty and socialising together in the bars. There is almost a feeling that everything and everyone else is superfluous – the airborne fraternity is autonomous in every sense. It is often said that 'the men of the brigade make it'. Certainly, they hold each other in high esteem and this is acknowledged by all ranks.

Soldiers are often as robust when letting off steam as they are when they are working and, as a result, there are occasional problems with the civilian community who find such spirited behaviour somewhat threatening. Some men make the point that they are expected and encouraged to be aggressive during their working day but are then penalised for rowdy behaviour when they are off duty. This is a recurring situation which continues to cause problems at times.

There are certain dates on the calendar that have special meaning for airborne forces. Arnhem Sunday and Rhine Crossing are celebrations of the brave deeds of 5 Airborne Brigade during the Second World War. They are commemorated with a church service followed by lunches to which veterans of the battle are invited. There is a great deal of pomp and ceremony where the Queen's and Regimental Colours are paraded and displayed with huge pride.

Drill and parades are regarded by paratroopers as a necessary evil, unlike other units of the army. However, on the fiftieth anniversary of the brigade, all airborne units rose to the occasion and paraded faultlessly at St Paul's in front of Prince Charles, their Commander-in-Chief.

A celebration for the whole family is Airborne Forces Day which takes place in the summer and is an all-day event. There are massed bands, march-pasts and displays and a host of military and fun sideshows to entertain the family. There is also a large beer tent which becomes a focal point as the day wears on and celebrations continue long into the night. For the officers, both serving and former, there is a large cocktail party in the evening, and there are many other functions throughout the brigade. Airborne Forces Day is a chance to catch up with old friends and you will find that many of the men who have left the regiment return to see familiar faces on this day.

Airborne social life plays its part in building a strong bond between the men and this trust serves them well in times of conflict. However, wartime affects the families and friends of servicemen as well. Apart from the obvious concerns for their partner's safety, which are considerable, in the case of the Falklands conflict many problems arose for airborne wives and girlfriends on their men's return. It was impossible for a wife fully to understand what her husband had been through and this often led to feelings of impotence or inadequacy. Having been the closest person in someone's life and then to find you are unable to communicate or help is a major obstacle for anybody to overcome. Naturally, because of the deep bonds between the men who fought together and the understanding brought about through mutual suffering, the veterans were more likely to speak to each other rather than to their partners,

Lenny gives Joe his
morning feed. Sadly,
many soldiers often
miss the milestone
moments in their
children's lives as they
are so often away on
exercise or tour.

A man's best friend ...
after his mucker.

if at all. And this was particularly true of the difficult period immediately after their return. Some men rejected their wives completely and others turned temporarily to drink and other outlets to relieve their frustration. The repercussions of the Falklands conflict were many and varied, but suffice it to say that many relationships were tested to the full on the men's return from down South.

The story of one Falklands veteran, Sergeant Lenny Carver, and his wife, Denise, is fairly representative of what happened to many families at that time. Denise recounts the experience: 'For the wives, it's a different kind of awful to what the men went through. I was expecting our first baby and was five months pregnant when Len went away. Like many people, I'd never even heard of the islands. I was so upset that I went home to my mum after he left.

'While they were away, we got two or three letters from the regiment to let us know where they were but we got most of our information from the television. You tended to listen to anything that might give you a snippet of news but it was silly really because it only upset you. The regiment put on outings and Sunday lunches for the wives in Aldershot but I preferred to be at home with my family. In fact, I don't know how I would have got through it without them. Of course, the wives with children at school had to stay on their own, which must have been hard.

'We didn't get much information at all. Len got shot on Saturday, 14 June 1982, on Mount Longdon. Regimental headquarters preferred that someone from the regiment rather than the police came to tell me so a captain from 1 Para turned up at my parents' home on Sunday lunchtime. He didn't know that I was eight months pregnant, which was a bit of a shock for the poor man. All he could tell me was that Len had been wounded on the left side of his spine in his lower back. That was all I knew for a week. I couldn't cry at the time. It was three weeks before I heard any more and then I got a telegram from Len saying he was all right, that he had had two operations and that "I will see you soon". That's when I burst into floods of tears. He had a two-minute call from HMS *Uganda* and then he was flown home. Like most wives and families, I was very disappointed that we weren't allowed to meet or see them at the airport. It struck us as very unfair.

'I went straight to the hospital to see him. It was funny really because he was on the same ward and in the same bed as a year before when he had been hospitalised with a rugby injury. Except this time I didn't recognise him because he looked so ill. I would be all right for a few days and then I'd have another good cry and then be all right again.

'Len didn't want a street party and bunting because he had lost so many friends. He couldn't stay with me when James was born because he had so recently seen such a lot of pain and suffering. We named James after his best friend who had been killed. James was born on 18 July – a month after Len was shot.

'It was ages before Len told me about how he got injured. We wives couldn't comfort or help them because we couldn't understand what they had been through. He can talk about it better now but really you need to get them with their mates to hear the stories. Some of them are quite funny. You know, Len had saved up all his porridge rations so that when the assault on Port Stanley was over he could have a big celebration meal. After he was wounded and they were cutting his webbing off him, all he could say was, "They're stealing my porridge."

'A lot of marriages went through a hard time after the Falklands as they readjusted. Of course it was absolutely awful for the men but it was difficult for the wives too.'

Lenny Carver has now left the regiment and is working as a policeman. The decision to leave was not an easy one and he admits that although he does not regret it, he still misses elements of his life with the Paras. 'It was a bit strange at first,' he says. 'There's an adjustment period. I've been out two years now, but I still miss it. Denise misses the company – the other wives and the mess.' However, Len believes that all he learned in the army is being put to good use in his new career. He seems content with the police – 'I work with a good bunch of lads' – and obviously enjoys having more time with his family.

For the majority of marriages which survived the difficulties in the wake of the Falklands conflict, army life continues as normal. At the time of the original interview with the Carvers, Len was involved in another kind of conflict, in Northern Ireland with 3 Para. However, Denise agreed with many other 3 Para wives that, despite the dangers, they were happier in Belfast on the accompanied tour because they saw more of their husbands than they would normally. The knowledge that for two years, despite the occasional separation, the family will see each other most evenings is very welcome. Other couples felt that rather than put their families at risk, they would prefer them to stay in England and endure the separation. This is far from an ideal situation and it means that the men do not see their families very often. As Denise says, 'If you're an airborne wife, you have to bring your children up on your own because their fathers are never there.'

The decision to leave your family in relative safety or subject them to the possibly dangerous consequences of your job is a hard one to make and it is a further example of how being a soldier is inextricably entwined with family life.

One of the many moments alone for army wives.

4
HOT-WEATHER TRAINING
NO SWEAT!

Airborne soldiers can sleep at any time in any place. It's a skill they learn early on since they never know when they will next have the chance to rest. Sleep deprivation is a familiar state for Paras.

Hot-weather training is an important aspect of 5 Airborne's schedule and prepares the brigade for out-of-area tasks which are one of its main functions. If unrest in a foreign country makes it necessary to evacuate British nationals, for example, 5 Airborne troops would be called in to carry out the evacuation. It is therefore imperative that all members of the brigade are trained to operate in the various climatic

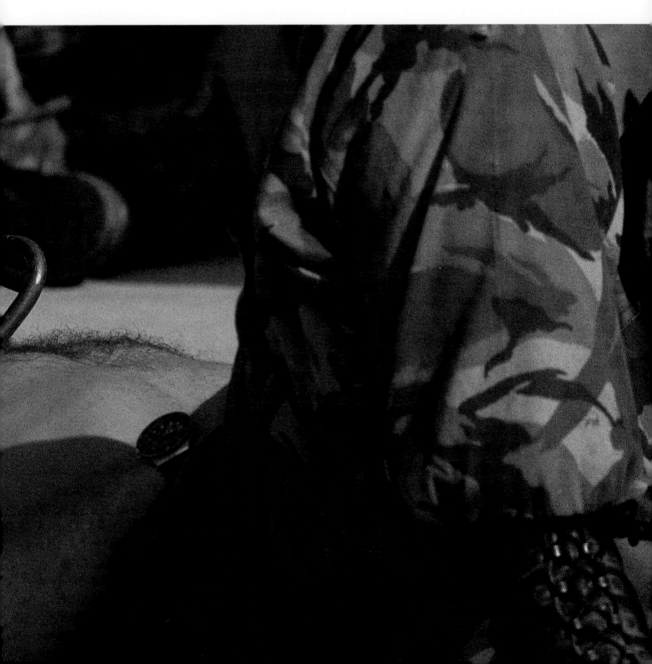

conditions they might meet in foreign territories, not least in the Third World.

Most of the overseas training grounds of the former British empire and colonies which were once used extensively by the British Army are no longer available, and opportunities for experiencing different types of climatic conditions are becoming more limited. Those locations still in use can roughly be broken down into arid and tropical categories and the training obviously varies accordingly.

TROPICAL TRAINING IN BELIZE Formerly British Honduras, Belize lies on the Caribbean (eastern) coast of Central America, bounded on the north and part of the west by Mexico and on the south and west by Guatemala. The inner coastal waters are shallow and sheltered by a line of coral reefs which extend almost the length of the country. The coastline is

Jungle patrols tend to be four-man units, self-sufficient and able to move quickly.

A 'march and shoot' live firing exercise in Belize.

dotted with islets called 'cayes', pronounced 'keys'. The low coastal plain is largely covered by mangrove swamps and the Maya Mountains form the backbone of the southern half of the territory. There are many rivers, some of them navigable for short distances by shallow-draught vessels, but a large proportion of the mainland is covered by dense forest or jungle.

The climate is sub-tropical and tempered by trade winds. At the height of the summer, temperatures can easily reach into the hundreds Fahrenheit in the interior although it is cooler in the coastal districts (up to about 96°F). As in all tropical climates, there are heavy rainfalls, particularly in the extreme south. Belize also suffers regular damage from hurricanes – the latest, in 1978, destroyed crops and caused widespread damage to roads, bridges and housing. These are the sort of conditions that 5 Airborne troops can expect when they arrive at Airport Camp for their four and a half month tour and jungle training.

Although Belize had been settled by the British since 1563, it was not until 1798 after a decisive victory over the Spanish that control of the settlement was properly established and in 1862 British Honduras was formally declared a British colony. In 1974, the country's name changed to Belize and independence was achieved on 21 September 1981. Close ties have been maintained with Britain and in the light of neighbouring Guatemala's continued territorial claim over Belize, the presence of British troops alongside the Belizean Defence Force (BDF) is welcomed. The BDF's expert knowledge of jungle survival is put to good use during the jungle training course.

In addition to the hot-weather infantry training value of Belize, the 9 Para Royal Engineer element of 5 Airborne also get the opportunity to put their specialist construction skills into practice. During their tour in 1989 they built six accommodation blocks in three months, plus a hangar for the BDF air wing, and carried out improvements to Airport Camp, including building a bar for the men. They also lent their skills to the Property Services Agency for construction work. The next year, 1990, saw a large-scale project for bridge-building in the area. This work is in addition to the jungle training and warfare course, the rudiments of which are much the same for all units of 5 Airborne.

JUNGLE TRAINING The jungle in Belize largely consists of secondary jungle which is denser than primary growth, and it is in these inhospitable surroundings that the exercises take place. Training is geared specifically to warfare but before that can start, each man must know how to survive. There is a saying that the 'jungle is neutral' but, as was proven in Vietnam, those who are familiar with it have a distinct advantage.

The men practise using high-frequency radio which is the

most appropriate form of communication in the jungle, albeit very difficult and unpredictable to operate. It tests initiative to the fullest and signallers have been known to climb trees with improvised antennae to get the best results. Because of the different atmospheric conditions and because jungle patrol areas are often surrounded by mountains, reception is hard to maintain, but it is vital to have radio communication since visibility is so impeded by dense foliage.

On average, it takes about four and a half hours to travel 800 metres through secondary jungle. So, moving operationally, a team might expect to cover only one or two kilometres in a day. However, in the Belizean scenario, many of the patrols are purposefully overt since it is intended that the local villagers tell their Guatemalan neighbours of the soldiers' presence to act as a deterrent and to have a reassuring effect on the local population.

The many rivers that snake through the Belizean jungle must be crossed on foot or swum. This is not always as easy as it sounds when one considers that each man is carrying a weapon and enough supplies to survive for several days. In addition, there are leeches and poisonous snakes to watch out for.

At the beginning of the course, the training group are shown how to build an A-frame shelter which offers some protection against the elements, although when moving operationally this would be a luxury, and the men would more usually make do with sleeping on the jungle floor or possibly in a rough hammock. The BDF instructor also explains how to extract water from plants and what can and cannot be eaten since the food supply to jungle patrols is often irregular. For example, the easiest way to get water in the jungle is to cut a vine. However, one particular vine variety is poisonous while another is safe to drink. Once you have identified which vine you have cut, the poisonous variety can then be used to catch fish by crushing the

Keeping alert through a river crossing. Apart from the dangers of poisonous snakes, the biggest nuisance of river crossings is the leeches. These have to be burned off.

cut end and dangling it in a pool. The poisonous juice causes fish to rise to the surface, so providing a meal – at least that is the theory.

In fact there is no shortage of water in the jungle and the men are equipped with Millbank bags to purify the natural supply by killing bacteria and filtering out solid matter such as animal faeces. It is perilously simple to contract amoebic dysentery from water if an animal dies upstream or local villagers use it as a latrine, so the Millbank bag must be used at all times, however inviting and clear the water may appear. Unfortunately, the water tastes vile after filtration through a Millbank bag.

These are all survival techniques which the trainees are taught before they venture into the jungle. The other preliminary is a safety lecture from the medical detachment. This covers health and hygiene, water discipline and what to do in the event of malaria or snake bites. This is not as unlikely as it may sound. In 1990, a visiting brigadier was bitten by a snake and was very seriously ill, almost losing his leg. The lecture also gives practical instruction on heat exhaustion and applying drips, a skill which was used extensively by the Toms in the Falklands.

An injury in the jungle during an operation is a very serious matter and casualty evacuation procedures must be understood and rehearsed. If the casualty is in a critical condition, an area large enough for a helicopter to come in and land would have to be cleared by the rest of the patrol, which is no mean task considering the density of the undergrowth. A minor injury requires a shelter for the casualty, clearing a winch-hole and marking the site with a marker balloon so that the helicopter can winch up the injured man and take him to safety. Once the helicopter has evacuated the casualty, then the rest of the men must move away as quickly as possible to avoid detection by the enemy. In extreme cases, a casualty is left as comfortably as possible and the base is radioed for help while the patrol continues with its task.

Navigation requires great concentration and determination, not to mention considerable confidence in map- and compass-reading abilities, since these are the only navigational tools available. Visibility in the jungle is negligible. It also takes several days to grow accustomed to sleeping in the jungle because there is great deal of unfamiliar and disconcerting animal noise at night. A popular trick that is frequently played on an unsuspecting young soldier is to place some food on his chest as he sleeps. The nightwalker monkey scavenges for food at night and the unfortunate victim wakens in a panic as the monkey jumps onto his chest to steal the food.

Posing a more serious threat are the numerous snakes which abound in the jungle. Not many species are deadly although a man would be very ill if bitten by any of the venomous varieties. Those that are highly poisonous such as the Ferd-i-Lance (it has green, white and yellow hoops and is territorial so it may attack without provocation) can kill a man within twenty-four hours if he does not receive medical assistance. Other natural dangers include scorpions and poisonous spiders. Leeches, although not life-threatening, are an uncomfortable and unpleasant nuisance which can be removed with a flame, cigarette or chemical remover. Most of the men become fairly adept at removing leeches – the ubiquitous Zippo lighter comes into its own in the jungle – and learn to cope with the various dangers and irritations, but the jungle is not a relaxing or comfortable place in which to linger.

The training progresses to close quarter battle (CQB) practice and the hardest part of this exercise is actually spotting the targets. Trainees cut a path through the jungle with machetes and then staff place targets on either side of the track. The trainees patrol on their own initially and then in pairs. Of the ten or twelve targets, they usually spot about half. You can pass a matter of only feet away from a motionless person and not see them in the dense foliage.

The course culminates in a four-day tactical phase. It puts into practice everything that the trainees have learned during the past six days and although all say they enjoyed it with hindsight, at the time it is a fairly nerve-wracking experience. The trainees spend the first night in hammocks in a cleared area. In the morning, they are sent out on recce patrols for a night ambush. The recce continues throughout the day until about 1600 hours when they move into ambush position where they stay until it is sprung. At first light (about 6 a.m.), staff and the BDF move through the position and are ambushed by the waiting men. The trainees have spent the whole night without moving in the heart of the jungle, equipped with nothing but the clothes they are wearing. All found it an uncomfortable and unnerving experience.

The following day they do further recces for a camp attack. After an evening meal, they move to position about a hundred metres from the camp that they intend to attack. They lie there quietly all night, again with only the kit and webbing that they carry. This demands 50 per cent alertness, which means half the group sleep while the other half observe. In reality, many find it impossible to sleep in these unfamiliar and hostile surroundings. At first light, they attack the camp.

The next day is devoted to personal administration and there is a non-tactical period during which medics can sort out blisters, sores and assorted jungle ailments. The development of proper jungle boots has done a great deal to alleviate the common problem of blisters and, with the right precautions, this painful soldiers' blight can largely be avoided on jungle training. Patrols are sent out for water and the soldiers have a short time to sort themselves out and prepare for the final exercise.

In the dense jungle foliage, a man can pass only a matter of feet from a stationary adversary without seeing him.

On the third night, trainees are given a 500-metre-square area to clear by first light. In normal circumstances, there is no movement in the jungle at night because it is so easy to get lost and because it is impossible to move quietly and without detection. Staff acting as enemy are left in the area waiting to be found and they also observe the group's progress. This is the end of the exercise and the patrol then tabs back to camp. There is a great sense of achievement at the end of the course and it is the one aspect of a Belizean tour that receives universal praise.

Throughout the final four-day tactical phase, the trainees are deliberately starved of sleep since this could quite possibly happen in a live situation. For the duration of the ten-day course, there is no washing or shaving. This may appear an unnecessary deprivation but it is sound practice, for scented toiletries and clean bodies only attract the bugs and mosquitoes in jungle conditions.

The jungle is better suited to small groups of operating troops because it is difficult to feed large numbers off the land. When a group are detailed to recce an area, a patrol base or harbour area is usually set up first. Observation patrols and ambushes are then sent out from there. The patrols find out information about the area and watch roads, bridges and tracks. The aim is to collate as much information as possible and then extract operational requirements from the gained intelligence. Small patrols work very much alone and react according to the information they gain in an operational jungle situation. The majority of men enjoy this element of the course because it gives them a chance to work on their own initiative away from superiors' watchful eyes.

As seems to be the case wherever they go, airborne soldiers managed to adopt a pet even in the improbable environment of the jungle – in this case a boa constrictor called Fluff which 3

Para acquired. It was rumoured that Fluff was on the ration roll and was allowed B$12 per week for his chicken diet. Predictably, someone got drunk one night and released him back to the jungle in a *Born Free*-inspired gesture.

A pet-loving patrol from 2 Para also returned to camp with a live reptilian trophy in someone's bergen after taking copious photographs in the jungle with the snake draped round their necks. On closer inspection, however, it was discovered that this was no sleepy boa but a Ferd-i-Lance – the most dangerous snake in Belize. Needless to say, the snake was rapidly removed and it is believed that it was only the fact that the snake had recently gorged itself on a large prey that saved the remarkably lucky members of the patrol.

BOAT PATROLS   A key function of the British presence in Belize is to patrol the many rivers in the south, including the Sarstoon which forms part of the border with Guatemala. The main purpose is to see and be seen and to pose a deterrent to the ever-watchful Guatemalans. In many areas the vegetation is too dense for vehicle patrols anyway, and even some of the rivers are too densely vegetated for boats to pass successfully and the narrower waterways remain unnavigable.

The boats used by 5 Airborne Brigade are Rigid Raiders; they have a shallow draught, are extremely fast and can outrun most of the drug smugglers in the area with a 45-knot top speed. They can also be transported on the back of a 4-ton lorry equipped with lifting gear. Wherever possible, boats are inserted and extracted in fresh water to prevent corrosion from seawater. They are used in sea conditions to reach the small cayes which serve as observation posts and adventurous training centres but it is a very rough ride for passengers as the Rigid Raider tends to plane across the water and then slam heavily into the troughs between the waves.

To patrol the rivers of
Belize, the army use
Rigid Raider vessels
which have a shallow
draught and a fast turn
of speed. This is the
Moho river.

The Rigid Raider is not a war boat as such. It can hold four to six armed men depending on how much equipment they are carrying and is often used for inserting men quickly and quietly into positions under the cover of nightfall. During a tour of Belize, they are more likely to be used to transport men on R&R (rest and recreation) and it is great fun and a test of nerve to lob off the side as they travel at speed through the water.

Soldiers are armed when patrolling the Sarstoon river which is overlooked by armed Guatemalan observation posts but, in the main, when patrolling the Rio Grande, Moho or the Temash rivers, the purpose is to reassure the local inhabitants and to gather information from remote villagers. Some of these settlements can only be reached by river and it takes villagers at least a day to reach the town in their crude dug-out canoes. Villagers warmly welcome the visits from soldiers who are virtually the only people to bring them news from the outside world. The villagers lead a very basic life, existing on a subsistence diet in their open thatched huts. But, ironically, they can usually manage to rustle up a bottle of Coke for honoured guests, as long as you return the refundable bottle before you leave.

In general, Belize is a popular tour and the men enjoy exploring the country and relaxing at the cayes in their leisure time. Many take the long bus ride into Mexico on R&R to taste the more sophisticated delights of some of the seaside resorts. Wives often 'indulge' out (subsidised air travel for military personnel and families on RAF planes) to spend two weeks with their husbands in this beautiful and fascinating country.

ARID TRAINING IN CYPRUS Cyprus is an island in the east Mediterranean which was ceded to Britain by Turkey in 1878. It was made a colony in 1925 but in 1955 Greek EOKA terrorists started a campaign for Enosis (Union with Greece)

Airborne soldiers make a point of visiting remote villagers and bringing them news from the outside world.

and the Parachute Regiment were called in to augment the island's security forces and mount anti-terrorist operations. Cyprus became an independent republic in 1960 but in 1964, following an escalation of political violence between the rival Greek and Turkish factions, the United Nations Truce Force took over the task of keeping Greek from Turk from 1 Para who had been called in to calm the situation earlier in the year. Following a Greek-supported military coup, the island was invaded by Turkey in 1974, leading to the virtual partition of the island with the Turks holding the northern sector. This uneasy situation continues unaltered. The southern Greek sector is used by 5 Airborne troops for training purposes. Although they have no direct interface with the UN peacekeeping troops stationed in Cyprus, this is a role that representatives of 5 Airborne have played on several occasions.

As opposed to Belize, where tours are usually a minimum of six months, Cyprus is close enough to be used for exercises of only a few days or weeks. When training in areas such as Cyprus, procedures for ambush and attacks do not vary tactically but certain provisions must be made to accommodate the extreme temperatures. Each man must carry extra water rations, for example, which adds to the already heavy load each must bear in the debilitating heat. Wherever possible, long-distance travel on foot is only attempted during the cool of the night or early morning and strenuous work is avoided in the full heat of the day, although these precautions are not always observed. The problem with travelling at night is that the terrain is particularly rough with rocky ravines and it seems that every plant in Cyprus is covered in sharp thorns. Movement by day is difficult enough and at night it is obviously complicated still further by not being able to see the treacherous terrain ahead, which leads to twisted ankles and similar injuries.

In medical terms, there should be a period of acclimatisation when arriving in areas of extreme temperature but on a military exercise which lasts only a matter of weeks, this is a rare luxury. However, maintaining high levels of exertion without a period of acclimatisation attracts the inherent dangers of heat stroke, heat exhaustion and their associated problems. All the men are trained to spot the early warning signs and during a 1 Para,

C Company intersection competition, most section commanders recognised and stopped any team member suffering from the heat at a very early stage. Yet there are inevitably some casualties requiring the medical staff's attention when men have to work hard in high temperatures under a fierce sun. Obviously, those of a fair or sandy complexion suffer more than others. If the casualty is not too bad, after a brief period of rest he will be used on exercises again as the enemy, taking care to ensure that he is not exposed to the sun at all.

Blisters pose another great problem to the men when exercising in hot climates. These are hard to avoid when running with weight across rough terrain with sweaty feet. Some men take the standard precaution of covering their feet with talcum powder before setting off and wearing two pairs of socks. There are numerous suggestions to avoid blisters but no matter what precautions are taken, by the end of a hard march and

Helicopters are sometimes used to evacuate troops from an exercise.

A timed run with heavy weight in the scorching heat of the Cyprus sun.

shoot competition, virtually every man's feet are in poor shape. Unfortunately, the common blister is far more hazardous in a hot climate where there is always a risk of infection.

Brief tours in hot climates are frequently used to test stamina and fitness and the resourcefulness of soldiers. Rather than doing straight eighteen-kilometre endurance marches in the heat (although these are also practised), competitions are often devised as a means of testing various skills that might one day be called upon operationally in a similar climate and environment. A two-day competition may comprise command tests that evaluate medical, signals and basic infantry skills over

The exhausting heat
takes its toll on the
men. Everyone lends a
hand to help those in
difficulty.

an eighteen-kilometre course where teams tab between events under the double difficulty of lack of sleep and extreme heat. The second day could be a march and shoot competition where the teams are initially inspected for personal management standards, that is to say, at the end of the first gruelling day when they are exhausted, the men still have to find the energy to clean their equipment spotlessly and wash and shave the following morning before starting the second part of the event. The entire two-day event is timed against the clock to increase pressure still further.

Prizes for such a competition frequently involve being excused some future exercise or guard duties. However, it is not the prize that goads men through the hardships of the event but pride in themselves and their section. It is clear by the end of the first day which teams stand a chance of winning such a competition but the amount of effort put in by every team on the final day is immense. Men who have been close to exhaustion and whose feet are in tatters at the end of the first day will put in a superlative performance during the second leg and push themselves to the limits of their physical endurance even though they cannot possibly win. This sort of effort cannot be accredited to incentive but purely to pride, determination and *esprit de corps*.

There are certain lessons to be learned from these arduous exercises and competitions. The sergeants, corporals and senior Toms have the benefit of experience on their side and they will advise the less seasoned soldiers on how to survive the heat. Yet no matter how much they stress the importance of not going out on the beer the night before an exercise, of eating breakfast and of sipping lots of water throughout the day, some of the younger men still refuse to heed the warnings. These are the ones who usually suffer from heat-related illnesses during the strenuous events; it is a hard lesson that is driven home in the most unpleasant manner. Once someone has experienced the disagreeable effects of collapsing through heat exhaustion and the ensuing muscle cramps in the legs, he will not make those mistakes again.

There is arguably a fine balance between the training benefits that can be reaped from these exercises and competitions and the disadvantages of increased injuries and heat-related casualties and their effect on morale. Officers sometimes exhibit a reluctance to alter their plans or to be seen to be too lenient and this leads to exercises continuing when it would perhaps be more prudent to stop and change tactics. The men do not mind working hard on an exercise if they are given time off afterwards in recognition of their efforts. Unfortunately, this is not always forthcoming.

One of the benefits of exercising in hot climates is that the adventurous training element of the tour tends to be more interesting and far more pleasant than in a colder climate. These locations lend themselves to all the water sports, and rock climbing is usually available in mountain regions. Trained instructors give lessons and advice on dinghy sailing, canoeing, wind-surfing and other sports and the main complaint is that there is never long enough truly to master and enjoy the activity.

On night exercise in
Cyprus.

5
NORTHERN IRELAND
KEEP YOUR HEAD DOWN

In August 1969, the Royal Ulster Constabulary accepted that they were unable to contain violence in Belfast and Londonderry without assistance and so the British Government agreed to deploy troops from bases in Northern Ireland and the mainland. Until this time the British Army had maintained a basic garrison of some 2,500 men in Northern Ireland but in 1969 troops were moved over from the mainland and twelve

Soldiers leave the base, bomb-bursting through the gate in South Armagh.

months after the first soldiers arrived on the streets, the total strength stood at 13,000. At the height of the troubles in 1972, when 103 soldiers were killed, there were over 21,000 regular soldiers in the Province. This figure stabilised at around 10,000 in 1986 and has been maintained around this level ever since.

When the troops were called in, the General Officer Commanding (GOC), Northern Ireland, assumed responsibility for all security operations, including those previously carried out by the police. This situation continued until 1977 when the RUC, now reorganised, strengthened and supported by the reserve force, once again took the lead in security matters under a policy called 'The Way Ahead' which re-established police primacy. While the army's role is now one of supporting the police, extremely close liaison continues between the two forces on all aspects of security operations. However, the police deliberately take a more high-profile image and are seen to be 'in the driving seat'.

The Parachute Regiment and 5 Airborne forces have played an active role in the Province from the outset, a deep and sometimes bitter involvement.

An official definition of the army's role is that 'soldiers are in Northern Ireland to support the police and to help prevent bloodshed and violence; to make it a safe place for people to live. The job includes searching for illegal arms and explosives and protecting the people against gunmen, bombers and other terrorists.' In fact, the role played by airborne forces is very much more complex although this forms the basis of their presence there. Tours of duty are either residential, which used to mean two years in permanent barracks and married quarters, accompanied by families, or roulement tours of four and a half months without the families. Despite intensive workloads, these periods have now been extended to a nearly three-year residential tour and six-month roulement tour.

Soldiers on patrol have to be constantly vigilant.

ROULEMENT TOUR IN SOUTH ARMAGH

Before troops are inserted on roulement tour, a plan is set up determining how to run the operation. As one colonel explained, 'Working on RUC advice and local knowledge, activities are planned to achieve a particular objective during the tour. However, in addition to attaining such aims, the unit must always be in a position to react to a situation and cover it in security terms.' This requires measure and counter-measure and an intensive workload for all.

In contrast to the normal army practice of living by routine, in the Province soldiers must deliberately live life without pattern. Unpredictability is a byword for survival. The only constant is the fact that each soldier, irrespective of rank, has only five days' leave during the six-month period and there is virtually no time off and no drinking. Since all soldiers draw an extra allowance when serving in Northern Ireland and, if married, receive separation money as well, one of the few benefits is that most men manage to save a good deal during the tour. It is grudgingly recognised as a highly successful, involuntary saving scheme.

Those working in the offices as clerks are also more busy on a roulement tour of Ireland. The Operations Room at Bessbrook Mill (Battalion HQ) is manned twenty-four hours a day and the watchkeeper sits at his desk constantly during his duty.

In South Armagh, all army movement by roads is reduced because of the threat of terrorist ambushes and planted bombs. Travel by personnel and the delivery of supplies are mostly carried out by helicopter. This causes a huge logistical problem every day for Buzzard who controls helicopter deployment. Planning is completed well in advance once all requests for helicopters have been received. Together with Operations (Ops), Buzzard decides what takes priority and a schedule is worked out. Naturally, if emergencies occur, the timetable is rescheduled; flexibility is the name of the game. These men manage to remain remarkably unflustered under enormous pressure and an immense number of variables. Despite innumerable last-minute alterations to their plans, they still bounce back with the apt catchphrase, 'I'm a rubber duck – you can't break me.'

Accommodation during these unaccompanied tours is crowded and of a fairly poor standard. At camps such as Forkhill, Crossmaglen and Newtownhamilton, it is not unusual to find six men sharing a room scarcely 8 feet by 8 feet – not that they spend much time there. The demands of the job mean they do little more than sleep in their rooms. Living in such close proximity, no one can be ignored and problems tend to be sorted out very quickly. Despite working long hours in frequently dirty conditions, soldiers have to be even more fastidious than usual regarding personal hygiene. If someone has a personal problem, he is soon told.

In Aldershot, each man takes pride in maintaining his own level of fitness and, in addition to the army physical training, most men can be seen going for regular runs in the locality. However, in South Armagh the men are confined to cramped and over-crowded camps for security reasons. They are unable to go for runs outside the boundaries and fitness levels rapidly fall off. Sitting in an observation post (OP) for five days without any exercise results in still further loss of fitness. To combat this, most camps and even the OPs have a small multi-gym and running machine set up for off-duty use and this equipment is used exhaustively. Strength training is maintained to some extent on patrols as each man sets off with a bergen and equipment usually weighing in excess of 100lb in order to be self-supporting for some days.

The abnormally high workload and long separation from family and friends often result in a period of low morale towards

Troops are inserted into, and picked up from, rural Observation Posts (OPs) by helicopter. However, demands for transport and inclement weather mean that men can be stuck at OPs for longer than anticipated.

the middle of the tour. Spirits tend to lift in the second half of the stay as the end comes within sight.

Each camp has a Quick Reaction Force (QRF) which is on hand to be deployed immediately in an emergency. They are equipped with two days' supplies and they work a twenty-four-hour stag. Most of the team rests or sleeps while at least one member of the group stays alert to take emergency calls. The QRF can be called out at any time for any number of reasons, from helping the police to unloading an underslung load from a helicopter. Similarly, there is an Air Reaction Force (ARF).

The men spend in the region of ten days on duty in camp. This includes town patrols and guards duty (manning barriers, guard rooms, sangars and QRF or ARF). When not on these essential but somewhat mundane duties within the camps, the men are either on rural patrols or manning observation posts.

RURAL PATROLS It is probably accurate to say that rural patrols are the favourite aspect of the roulement tour. It is what the men are trained for and, especially for the subalterns (junior officers) and NCOs, it is a great proving ground away from the scrutiny of senior ranks. Men and officers alike welcome the opportunity 'to do their own thing' and, moreover, to do it well. Everyone seems supremely confident in this particular milieu and, despite the physical hardships, most enjoy the challenge of putting sound training into practice.

As already mentioned, unpredictability is the key in this region and so patrols must vary the time they go out and the length and pattern of their movements. A patrol can last from a matter of days to weeks on the ground and the men only display themselves openly when necessary. During this period, they may well have a number of tasks to perform related to RUC requests to protect and support their activities. Whatever their function, they keep off the roads because these routes are predictable and invite ambush. This means that the patrol must walk across fields. Since they do not want to give away their final destination to possible observers, distances are rarely covered by a direct route. An added hindrance are the blackthorn hedges which are prolific in this part of Ireland. They are almost impenetrable and the sharp, hooked thorns can get through the thickest clothing. No one returns from a patrol unscathed.

Part of a patrol's function is to observe suspicious activity. In most cases, this is simply reported during the debrief session at the end of the patrol. In some instances, however, a difficult decision must be made as to whether to investigate and thus compromise those in the patrol or to stay undetected.

A patrol's aim is to leave the terrorist uncertain as to where they are and how many of them there are. Their presence may be suspected but not known for sure and it is this element of uncertainty that is hoped to deter the terrorists' movement of weapons and explosives. The Provisional IRA in particular have become extremely sophisticated and resourceful and they have developed elaborate methods for moving equipment using a series of cars and personnel. Confrontation is only likely to occur when a patrol intercepts some terrorist activity by chance or through gathered intelligence. Direct confrontations are rare and the rural conflict is far less overt than one might imagine. It is more a war of attrition.

One of the biggest dangers for the inexperienced soldier is falling into the trap of the 'come on'. In South Armagh, this is often in the form of an interesting piece of equipment left by the terrorists in a field which they hope might be picked up by an inquisitive soldier. It could well be booby-trapped. Alternatively, it may serve the purpose of a diversionary tactic while some more important activity is taking place elsewhere.

The learning curve in Northern Ireland is extremely steep for

All the training and
exercises come into
play in operational
patrolling in South
Armagh.

a young soldier and for some it is their first battalion experience. A soldier is under extreme stress and he knows that any error could cost him his life or that of his fellow men. This incessant pressure of responsibility and sure knowledge of the dangers that surround them makes patrolling in South Armagh a tense yet stimulating and exhilarating experience. For a young Tom, it also requires huge self-discipline to go into a location such as a wet, muddy ditch and stay there for days observing a given situation. As mentioned in Chapter Three, the relatively recent issue of Goretex (a breathable, waterproof material) kit has made this sort of task considerably more comfortable. Goretex socks, snow gaiters and bivvy bags now keep patrolling soldiers reasonably dry in most conditions short of crossing rivers which, unfortunately, is also often necessary.

Although there is limited contact with civilians on a rural patrol, soldiers may be required to assist the RUC in civil matters, so it is instilled in the young, aggressive airborne soldiers to exhibit a polite and civil manner to the local population in an effort to be a reassuring presence. It requires a high degree of professionalism to be able to maintain this approach 99.9 per cent of the time and yet produce an immediate, aggressive response on the rare occasion that it is required. By and large, civility is shown to the local population but there are times when a rather heavy-handed approach slips in.

True to form, the Paras managed to attract a motley collection of pets during the South Armagh tour. At Newtownhamilton, Gnasher the dog was very proud of the fact that he always managed to chase off any helicopters that landed in short order. He loved to follow patrols and this scruffy black mongrel could always be seen standing guard. Similarly, 1 Para were adopted by a dog at Forkhill, whom they christened Desmond Tutu. He accompanied most patrols and it eventually got to the stage

River crossings are an unpleasant, dangerous, yet integral part of rural patrols.

where soldiers would try and creep out without him because his presence gave them away.

OBSERVATION POSTS   Observation posts are either towers or mountain-top sites and, as the name suggests, their main function is to observe and monitor activity in a certain region, and thus restrict terrorist movement.

OPs tend to be sited in remote areas and close to the border between North and South. They are usually very basic in terms of facilities. All rations, water and supplies must be brought in by helicopter in large underslung nets. Tower OPs (the vast majority) consist of a glass and wooden box swaying around at the top of a 70-foot gantry and accommodation/recreational space is dug in underground. In fact, everything is underground including toilets, shower and a small multi-gym so that the men can work out and attempt to maintain fitness levels since there is no opportunity to run. Conditions are cramped and the atmosphere is musty with a team of four to six men in each curtained room. There is a communal 'rest' room with a television and video and a small kitchen. Relations have to be good when you are living in such close proximity and an even greater camaraderie frequently develops among the men.

In general, soldiers spend around twelve days at an OP and since the platoon is detached from the rest of the company, it is a good opportunity for a lieutenant (platoon commander) to work independently and prove his worth. Despite the crowded environment and lack of creature comforts, the men appear to prefer the relative freedom of the OP to guard duties back at camp. It is a punishing schedule of four-hour shifts which often means working a sixteen-hour day either in the OP itself or in the QRF role. This is a very busy function: QRF duties cover responsibility for unloading deliveries from helicopters, sand-bagging, cleaning, sangar duties and so on.

Tower OPs look unstable and sway unnervingly in the wind, but they have been known to withstand mortar and other attacks.

The OP is in constant radio communication with the accommodation area and a team commander or the platoon commander can be contacted at any time. Observers in the tower are alert to changes in routines or unusual behaviour. Watching the same landscape day in and day out ensures that each man becomes familiar with daily routines and they learn the features of the land by heart. The vast majority of what they see is normal farm work and this duty can become very monotonous but they must be constantly vigilant for anything out of the ordinary.

The tower is usually in a good defensive position and it is armed. In fact, several tower OPs have withstood mortar attacks despite their flimsy appearance. Unfortunately, because of the nature of an OP, their position is often virtually inaccessible. The only means of transport in or out is by helicopter and with the renowned inclemency of Irish weather, groups of men are often stranded at an OP for far longer than the anticipated period.

The 'troubles', as Northern Ireland's internal strife is euphemistically called, seem strangely out of place in the beautiful scenery of South Armagh. There are only small, isolated pockets of unrest but it produces a rather surreal atmosphere to see the scars of bomb damage in such stunning natural beauty. Geographically, the district works against the army. The tracks and routes used by smugglers to cross the border are almost too numerous to count and Republican support in certain areas guarantees the troops a hostile reception with little or no co-operation. Nonetheless, the indigenous people are war-weary and many want an end to the twenty years of turbulence. They tolerate an army presence and feign indifference, which is the safest route for those living constantly in the midst of violence.

The all-pervasive threat and pressing workload of a six-month

Utrinque paratus - ready for anything.

unaccompanied tour means that officers and men must pull together. Young officers lean heavily on their NCOs and seasoned Toms for guidance and everyone is generally more supportive of those around them. The men, particularly those on their first NI tour, seem to love the challenge and opportunity to prove themselves and are excited by the chance 'to see some action', as it is often put. 'It's the nearest thing to war' is how one young soldier explained it. Naturally, wives, girlfriends, friends and families are sorely missed by all but although everyone is tired by the end of the tour, the general consensus seems to be 'that this is the only time you get to do it for real, so do the business'.

This kind of tour thrusts a lot of responsibility on every man, regardless of rank. Needless to say, it matures the younger men very quickly, and constant company and shared dangers mould men together, producing an impressive unity.

There is no time for complacency or even complete relaxation in off-duty moments. Crossmaglen was mortared shortly before our arrival. Fortunately, no one was injured, although there was considerable material damage. The attack was mounted at the heart of the camp, despite the presence of observation sangars at the boundaries.

RESIDENTIAL TOUR IN BELFAST The style of a residential urban tour is very different to that of the rural short roulement. In an urban environment the deterrent is a reassuring presence and so high visibility is required. Because wives and families are with the men and the workload is less intense, it is easy to imagine that the pressure is less. However, the threat is far more insidious; it is difficult to stay vigilant for nearly three years and it becomes tempting to adopt a more relaxed approach, yet the dangers are no less real. Naturally, soldiers and their families want to live as normal a life as

A rolling vehicle checkpoint (VCP) in South Armagh receives a mixed response from local residents. This soldier may appear to be alone, but the patrol has blended into the background.

possible but there are certain precautions which must be taken and it would be irresponsible to pretend that a threat does not exist.

The battalion and its families are based at a large camp which includes accommodation, medical centre, churches, sports facilities, swimming pool and shops. A family could probably live on the camp for the duration of the tour and never venture beyond its gates. However, for the soldiers, although a lot of work is centred here, the patrol area is in the higher risk parts of the town centre and West Belfast.

The 3rd Parachute Battalion were on tour from 1989–91. They were replaced in February 1991 by 1 Para, and 2 Para will take over from them in early 1993. They fulfil the role of Province Reserve, which means the battalion has no direct area of control but supplies men to other units where necessary. This results in a restricted area of activity for the commanding officer and his senior ranks, which they find frustrating. A CO in Northern Ireland is unlikely to parachute with his battalion, run exercises or truly command. His is a nominal role. By contrast, in a similar way to the rural tour, company and platoon commanders have many opportunities to test their skills during a residential tour.

When troops are based at the camp, frequently working twenty-four hours on followed by twenty-four hours off, they perform all the standard guard duties plus additional driving duties, providing escorts for vehicle movements and conducting occasional vehicle checkpoints (VCPs) in the general vicinity of the camp. Although not as pressured as South Armagh, the work schedule is still hectic. Those who are accompanied by their families have the benefits of seeing them most evenings, if at a somewhat late hour. However, for those men whose girlfriends are back on the mainland, it can be many months between visits. It is difficult for girlfriends to visit their loved ones in

Northern Ireland and leave periods are infrequent. Unfortunately, a residential tour in Belfast often sounds the death knell for many relationships.

During patrol duties, soldiers may have to carry weapons such as a revolver, which they would not normally carry on the mainland. On camp, therefore, all soldiers must undergo additional weapon training. There is also a renewed emphasis on fitness training, including daily sessions at the gym and circuit training. A brisk run round the camp is a normal part of the daily routine. The fitness schedule is supplemented by team sports, mainly soccer or rugby, and swimming; during the men's time off, the squash courts are also in constant use. Each accommodation block has a multi-gym and these are well used – many spend most of their spare time working out and keeping fit. During the 1 Para tour, the CO led a regular 6.30 a.m. beasting session – a gruelling experience – twice a week throughout the tour.

Whereas in the rural environment the men feel that this is what they were trained for, in a supportive policing role in a city environment, more scepticism prevails about the appropriateness of the airborne soldier's specific skills. There is a distinct sense of frustration that their responsibilities are limited. Nonetheless, there is no doubt that every man goes about his duties with complete professionalism and privately voiced reservations are not aired outside the camp. Fortunately, the working relationship with the RUC is generally good and efficient, although there is a certain amount of caution on both sides.

Unlike South Armagh, helicopters are not used to such a wide extent and movement of personnel is made by road, although helicopters do have a role to play. For road movement, men are usually moved in armoured personnel carriers (APC, or Pigs as they are more familiarly known). These tend to move in small

Operational tours also require soldiers to be crack shots with a pistol.

convoys and, since there have been several attacks by the IRA using Russian anti-tank weapons, once again unpredictability is essential. A different route and various timings must be used whenever possible, although in a built-up area the number of routes by road to a particular destination are limited.

At any one time, a company of men is usually attached to an RUC police station in order to support their activities and to perform patrols. This is usually in what is known as a 'hard' area such as the Falls Road, Divis Flats or White Rock. During these six-week attachments, the officers and men live in very similar conditions to those of the South Armagh camps and work at a similar intensity with shorter, more frequent patrols. Conditions are cramped and accommodation is basic with six men sharing a small space and sleeping in three-tier bunks. The cookhouse stays open twenty-four hours a day so that night patrols can prepare something hot for themselves on their return. Recreation space is severely limited but a lively and often raunchy range of videos are cabled through to the television room. Officers and senior NCOs have a small common room with tea and coffee facilities and a larger television but otherwise accommodation is not much different. As in South Armagh, these stations are not safe from assault and mortar attacks are not uncommon. The attacks are usually aimed at those RUC stations in the heart of pro-Republican territory and this is frequently where the soldiers are called upon to patrol.

URBAN PATROLS Since most of the army's work involves supporting the RUC, there is a close liaison between the Ops room and the RUC administration. An RUC officer will conduct his routine duties – delivering summonses, paying house calls and other standard police work – accompanied by a number of soldiers, who are there primarily to guard him. They also assist him in such procedures as VCPs where road blocks

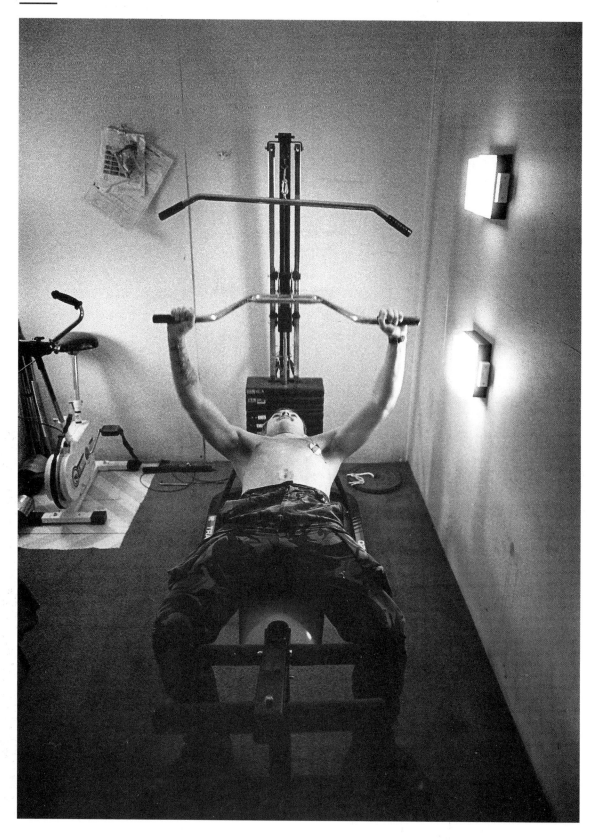

Keeping fit in an
Observation Post is
difficult, as there is
little scope for physical
training. Most OPs now
have small multi-gyms
to help keep the men in
condition.

are set up at random and cars are stopped in order to search for
anything unusual and to check the driver's documents and
papers (unlike the mainland, Northern Ireland citizens carry
identity papers). Anything that strikes the soldiers as suspicious
or unusual is noted and the car's details are checked.

The public's response to VCPs is usually one of resignation
and most Belfasters accept that it is a necessary evil. However
there will always be the odd awkward customer who becomes
abusive and the soldiers must learn to tolerate these verbal
attacks. Forbearance is a quality not normally associated with
airborne troops. The checkpoints are not maintained for too
long since news travels fast and stationary soldiers and RUC
men make easy targets.

The numerous hours
spent confined to an OP
are filled by endless
videos.

On occasion, the most dangerous encounter the soldiers will
meet is that of a soiled nappy being dropped on them from the
flats above. This is a smelly and unpleasant experience but it

becomes far more ominous when refrigerators start to land on them.

Patrols are mounted twenty-four hours a day and considerable groundwork, planning and briefing are carried out beforehand, with every effort being made to vary routes and procedures. Frequently, it is the night patrols that are most productive. The public, who are becoming increasingly disillusioned and unhappy with the terrorist situation, may be more

The army's role in Northern Ireland is to support police primacy. However, the two forces work very closely together.

Night patrolling in Belfast. This photograph was taken with the aid of an army image-intensifier weapon sight.

communicative at night when they cannot be seen by prying eyes. Radio contact becomes even more important since visibility is so restricted and night sights on weapons are used extensively for observation. As in all depressed areas, there are a large number of drunks on the streets at night but they rarely pay the soldiers any heed or cause any trouble. Groups of young men and girls stand idly on street corners and watch the patrol with mistrustful eyes in sullen silence. When patrolling in nice, suburban bungalow areas after the obvious dangers of a rough housing estate it is easy to be lulled into a false sense of security, but attacks are just as frequent in these apparently quiet backwaters and a soldier cannot afford to relax his guard at any time. Many young soldiers are surprised to learn that these 'nice' areas are the homes of the terrorist hierarchy.

In the daytime, the public are more reluctant to speak to the soldiers but this does not hold true of the children. As the patrol passes through shopping malls and housing estates, children always approach the soldiers and chat quite fearlessly to them, knowing full well that many carry sweets in their ration packs. Many ask to look through the sights of the gun and soldiers are mostly happy to oblige. In the vast majority of cases, this is

There is a temptation to relax when a patrol reaches a nice, suburban area, but these can also be dangerous and often contain the homes of known terrorists.

harmless curiosity but it has been known for children in 'hard' areas to make this request with the express purpose of altering the focus of the sight. In general, the children are merely inquisitive and looking for entertainment and distraction like those the world over, but their mothers are less keen on such fraternising and are often hostile. Many will pull their children

away if they find them talking to soldiers. There is a story, probably apocryphal, of the child who once said to a soldier, 'My uncle Johnny's got a gun just like this,' and an RUC investigation ensued.

The other local contact the soldiers have is with the numerous roaming dogs which bark at them incessantly. The entire patrol is usually conducted to the accompaniment of a howling, snarling canine chorus and it is commonly believed among the troops that Republican sympathisers train their dogs to bark at men in green.

The major source of abuse for the soldiers comes from women and adolescents. Youths have become very accurate at lobbing bricks from quite some distance and they are fully aware that the soldiers will not catch them if they chase after them because they cannot run fast in all their equipment. More importantly, the soldiers must always be aware of the come-on situation where they could be led up an alleyway into an ambush or miss a major event by these diversionary tactics. Women, on the other hand, prefer to lash the soldiers with their tongues and often tell them to 'go home and get out of our country. You're not welcome here.' Whether one agrees with their sentiments or not, there can be no doubt that their feelings are genuine and it is unfortunate that the soldiers must bear the brunt of their anger. Even the most war-hardened veteran finds it difficult to deal with verbally and physically abusive women.

The housing estates and blocks of flats of West Belfast do not differ greatly from the rough, underprivileged housing estates in any other part of Britain. The area is covered with refuse and graffiti, and broken and boarded windows are common even in inhabited homes. Everyday life continues, with kids playing in the streets and, as is the case wherever there is high unemployment, young men accompanying their wives and children on shopping expeditions or visiting relatives and

A whole generation of children in Northern Ireland have never known life without armed soldiers on their doorstep.

In Belfast, patrols are
part of everyday life.

friends. There is a constant flow of black taxis in and out of the area, for locals use the cabs as a public transport network. But there is a strangely oppressive feel that cannot solely be accredited to poverty. There is a constant feeling of hostile eyes being turned upon strangers and the tension of imminent trouble hangs in the air and is all-pervasive. Children nonchalantly kick a football against a wall that bears the scorchmarks from a recent IRA knee-capping incident, and families appear inured to the horrors of yet another sectarian killing in the area.

Soldiers are naturally edgy and constantly alert when patrolling in these areas. They never stand in one position in the open for too long and they are encouraged to develop a swaying motion even when stationary in order to lessen their chances of becoming a sniper's target. They soon become aware of warning signals such as a street emptying on their approach or telephones ringing in empty houses as they pass. They know that their every action is monitored and reported back to the

Dusk on a street patrol in Belfast.

terrorists by sympathisers called Dickers. As they move about, they check cautiously behind hedges and fences where explosive devices may be left and avoid passing close to lampposts and walls since bombs are often set at head height awaiting the careless soldier who passes too close.

Many of the younger men said that they were very nervous when they went on their first patrol but most became somewhat fatalistic after only a few sorties. To be as vigilant as possible is the only defence and, besides that, they must trust to thorough training and luck. The pre-Northern Ireland training that they received was generally considered excellent but, despite every precaution, members of the regiment have been killed over recent years.

After each patrol, there is a debrief session where information and observations are exchanged. Soldiers are encouraged to mention anything that struck them as unusual, however trivial it may seem, and some valuable and potentially life-saving information has been gleaned from such sessions.

Like those in South Armagh, the soldiers in Belfast reported that they most enjoyed the operational aspect of the tour. Again, the fact that they were doing the job and were left relatively to their own devices away from headquarters appealed to most of them. Every man in a platoon has to rely on his training to maintain the safety of the group and this collective responsibility produces a cohesive team who work well together for the common good and safety of them all. There are obvious frustrations for elite airborne soldiers performing a policing role and many express doubts as to their suitability, preferring to be operational where their specialised skills can be of value. However, in broad terms, the disciplined approach and professionalism that the Paras bring to the urban setting appear to produce good results in a sadly on-going situation of civil strife.

Overleaf: **Top cover sentries - a 1990s equivalent of riding shotgun on a stagecoach, only colder.**

INDEX